ENDEAN

Michael Burns.

ENDEAN

A South African Sportsman
in the Apartheid Era

Michael Burns

NIGHTWATCHMAN BOOKS

Nightwatchman Books
10 Selwyn Road, New Malden, Surrey KT3 5AT
0208 942 5588

in association with

Fairfield Books
17 George's Road, Bath BA1 6EY
01225 335813

First published 2017

ISBN: 978 0 9568510 7 9

Printed and bound in Great Britain by
CPI Antony Rowe, Chippenham, Wilts

Contents

This book is dedicated to the memory of

John Cope

Acknowledgements

This book was made possible largely thanks to extensive access to the Russell Endean family archive freely given to me by two of his children, Jane and Ross. My initial research took me to St John's College, Johannesburg, where history teacher Daniel Pretorius, cricket coach Adrian Norris and librarians Clifford Vaux and Angie Delport provided me with an enormous amount of help and information about Endean's childhood. I am particularly grateful to Clive van Ryneveld, Doug Insole and Robin Thorne who shared memories of playing first-class cricket with and against him. Trevor Quirk's monumental film history of South African cricket was an invaluable source: for both glimpsing Endean in action and for interviews with long-departed cricketers. For those who both read and edited drafts of the book, I am indebted to Mary Burns, Nick Humphrey and particularly to David Kynaston who gave his advice unstintingly throughout the whole writing of the book. Finally, I would like to thank Stephen Chalke for his generous expertise: as a cricket writer as well as his supervision of the design and production that has made the book a reality.

Prologue

Eighty-year-old weather guru Inigo Jones got his homespun forecast for the month of December 1952 absolutely right: Christmas Day in Melbourne was indeed a 96-degree scorcher. He correctly predicted much cooler weather for Boxing Day, with just a sprinkling of early-morning rain – it was the second day of the 1952 Second Test between Australia and South Africa. After a delayed start, Jack Cheetham's young and unfancied Springbok team, already one down in the series, were defending their meagre first innings total of 227, made on Christmas Eve. With only three fit bowlers, but backed up by some dazzling catching and ground fielding, the visitors were sticking doggedly to their task. But, with late afternoon sunshine casting long shadows across the vast open spaces of the MCG, and with dashing hometown hero Keith Miller on 52 and starting to dominate, things were slipping away from the South Africans. The tall dark-haired all-rounder, who had already struck bespectacled leg-spinner Percy Mansell for one mighty six, next turned his attention to metronomic off-spinner Hugh Tayfield. The on-drive was perfectly struck; but, as the 24,000 crowd rose to greet another six, the athletic figure of Russell Endean ghosted smoothly anti-clockwise around the boundary, both hands raised above his head to shade his eyes from the evening sun. Just as the huge hit was about to disappear into the cowering spectators, the green-capped out-fielder, with a graceful leap, miraculously clutched the speeding ball right-handed high above his head, coming down to earth with his back hard up against the ground's ornate wrought-iron railings. An earthy expletive exploded from the astonished Miller as he realised what had happened. The crowd was momentarily stunned, but then a mighty roar broke out, followed by sustained applause. While the retreating batsman with typical generosity applauded the wonder catch, Endean walked sheepishly towards the middle to be greeted halfway by his backslapping team-mates. In the ABC commentary box, Aussie broadcaster Johnny Moyes was beside himself: 'An incredible catch, a cricketing miracle, a feat which will never be forgotten, it will become part of cricket history!'

Chapter One

No Worries Now

While on a chilly Glasgow spring morning in 1924 the South African tourists were bowling out Scotland for an embarrassing total of just 36, five thousand miles away in Johannesburg Ella Endean was giving birth to her second son, William Russell Endean. His 'Geboortesertifikaat' (birth certificate) recorded that he was born on 31 May at Dundalk Avenue, in the city's Parkview district, his race given as 'European'. And on 3 August he was baptised into the Anglican Church of St George, Parktown by the Rev. Harold F Cranswick. His parents were both English immigrants: his father, William John, a Cornishman from St Austell; and his mother Ella (nee Walton), a Yorkshire lass, from Hebden Bridge. Russell's father was born into a mining family – on his 1888 birth certificate his own father (also William) had listed himself as a gold miner. The younger William was soon put to work underground himself, learning the special skills that had been passed down by Cornish miners through the centuries. But as the tin mining industry declined at the end of the nineteenth century, the Endean family decided to seek their fortune in the wider world. Drawn by the siren call of gold, they tried their luck as prospectors in Australia and New Zealand before settling in the fast-growing city of Johannesburg, where the young William worked as a miner in the giant Witwatersrand goldfields. However, by the time Russell was born, his father's days at the rock face were over; at the age of thirty-six he was now sitting behind a desk in the offices of Consolidated Goldfields. William and Ella Endean lived with their two sons Howard and Russell and their native servant Wilson on the corner of 4th Avenue and 5th Street on the Houghton Estate, a northern suburb of Johannesburg. William, following the practice of the affluent in this prosperous gold-mining city, had bought a generous piece of land on which he built his own exclusive detached property.

Russell, as he was always known, started his education, aged four, at the nearby Houghton Preparatory School; his first report gave him highest marks for 'Conduct' and 'Spelling' and lowest for 'Dutch', but accepted that he was 'only just commencing'. In the autumn of 1930 he joined his older brother Howard at the preparatory school of the prestigious St John's College – an establishment that was to become an abiding influence in his life. The school was founded in 1898 to educate the offspring of the hordes of prospectors who had descended on Johannesburg during the gold rush of 1886. After the traumatic upheavals of the Boer War the school had been re-founded for 'scholars of European descent', and in 1907, thanks partly to a £5,000 donation from the diamond magnate Thomas Cullinan, it moved to its present location on the Houghton Estate. The British architect Herbert Baker, responsible later for the Grace Gates at Lord's and for some of South Africa's most prominent buildings, designed the new school. Situated high up on a 'picturesque kopje', the simple but striking edifice was built with local rose-red quartz stone and looked down on extensive playing fields in the valley below. The young Endean went into 1b of the prep school aged six years and four months, a year younger than the class average. Despite suffering from diphtheria and missing 27 half-days through illness in his first year, his headmistress, Miss Thomas, wrote that he has made 'a very satisfactory beginning – a good boy'. Over the next three years he continued his steady but unremarkable course through the school; the most common assessment was that he was often 'careless and untidy', with his academic progress no doubt hampered by many more days of absence due to ill health – his records indicate that he missed 28 half-days during the 1935 Easter term alone. However, a sepia photograph from this period does not indicate that he was wasting away; it shows a chubby-faced, suntanned boy posing in the family's back garden with pimple gloves, grubby pads, black shoes and an unrefined batting stance. In another photograph of the school's 1st XI cricket team, he sits proudly in the captain's high-backed, bentwood chair, wearing white shorts and grey socks. His team won seven matches, drew one and lost two; the school magazine, *The Johannian*, noted that 'Endean proved a sound captain' and that his batting was 'invaluable'. On his final prep school report, the headmaster Mr Dobson, after complimenting him on his efforts on the cricket field, wrote: 'Our good wishes, and gratitude, go with him.'

****

At the end of December 1936 Russell Endean transferred to the senior school. Still a year younger than the rest of his form, the twelve-year-old new boy was put in Alston House, and started in the Lower IV form. St John's College, now one of the most influential private schools in twenty-first century South Africa, was during the worldwide depression of the 1930s struggling to attract pupils. Reflecting these hard times, the fees were modest. For the day boy Endean, the 1937 Easter term's fees, less allowances of 18/-, were £8.7s.0p; equivalent to just £250 in 2015 values (a term's fees in 2016 are approximately £2,400). As an Anglican foundation the school's pupils were expected to become formal members of the church, and on 27 November 1937 the Bishop of Johannesburg, Geoffrey Clayton, confirmed Russell Endean in the St John's College Chapel. Twenty years later, on the day before he died, Clayton, by then the Archbishop of Cape Town, would sign a letter refusing to implement section 29c of the Native Laws Amendment Act that sought to force apartheid in all Christian congregations.

Russell aged 9 in the Endean family's Johannesburg garden

The school, although exclusively white, made efforts to educate their pupils about living conditions of the 'Bantu peoples'. It invited external speakers such as Alan Paton (author of *Cry, the Beloved Country*) who talked about his work as head of the Diepkloof Native Reformatory; and the future anti-apartheid campaigner, the Rev. Trevor Huddleston, who spoke to the boys about the appalling overcrowding in the townships. The school did its bit for its less fortunate neighbours by supporting the Sophiatown Mission, a local organisation trying to teach 200 native children in one small, poorly equipped schoolroom. But, as Daniel Pretorious points out in his *History of Cricket at St John's College*, education for native Africans was a very low priority for the country's white politicians. He quotes a contribution in a 1938 edition of *The Johannian* by an unidentified author:

> The Government of South Africa does not foresee the advantage to itself and to the nation in proper native education. … It is often advocated that the native should be taught some useful trade or handicraft, and the "book-work" mainly left out. But what use is a trade when he is not allowed to practise it? There are no native trade unions in South Africa; any attempt in that direction is forbidden; and a native cannot by law practise any trade. … The only solution of the native problem [would be for the] future administrators of South Africa, educated in liberal and fair-minded traditions, [to] break down the Colour Bar, improve native education, and benefit South Africa by exploiting the mine of talent and ability up to now lying dormant.

'Alas,' laments Pretorious, 'in a time when centenary celebrations of the Great Trek were being exploited in the cause of Afrikaner nationalism, these views were largely ignored.'

While Endean's academic work was unremarkable during his first years at the school – it was routinely reported as either 'satisfactory' or 'quite satisfactory' by the headmaster, the Rev Sydney Herbert Clarke MA (Trinity College, Cambridge) – it was on the sports field where the diminutive but stocky boy stood out from the crowd. In 1937 and 1938 he was a member of Alston House's rugby and cricket teams that won four junior trophies. In the 1938 cricket competition Endean was picked out for special mention; and the next season, captaining the Alston's Junior XI, his team won the tournament 'thanks to a century by Endean'.

****

On 3 September 1939 Britain and France declared war on Germany; South Africa formally announced that it would join forces with the Allies a few days later. Immediately, several St John's teachers left the school to volunteer for military service. They were followed by several Old Johannians, amongst them Bruce Mitchell (1935 hero of South Africa's first Test victory against England), Ronnie Grieveson, Springbok wicketkeeper-batsman, and the prolific schoolboy batsman Owen Wynne who would play for South Africa after the war. Cricket (still being played on matting wickets) continued at St John's during the war years. In 1940, now a member of the senior Alston XI, Russell Endean featured in a very notable shield final against Hill House. The game was played as a 'timeless match', the same format as the Test between South Africa and England at Durban in the previous year – a match abandoned after ten days because the visitors, on 654-4 and only 52 runs short of victory, had to catch a boat home. In the St John's timeless final, Alston batted first and, in an opening partnership of 400 runs, Endean scored 183, his opening partner Mike Bold going on to score 354 in the team's eventual total of 813. Hill fell 339 runs short, being dismissed for 474 in what could be described as a 'batsman's match'. In the St John's 1st XI photograph from 1940, Endean sits wearing his maroon and dark blue striped blazer two seats from the grey-haired and moustached long-standing coach, Major Humphrey William Maghull Yates, a Wykehamist who, before serving in the First World War, had played for Hampshire as a dashing batsman and brilliant fielder for three seasons. This inexperienced 1940 team led by Bob Mitchell (brother of Bruce) had an unremarkable season, and the only notable score for the fifteen-year-old Endean, who was awarded his full colours in that year, was 51 in a losing cause against Jeppe High School.

The once sickly prep-school boy was now a healthy five-foot-ten-inch, well-built, all-round teenage sportsman – in the winter months he excelled at rugby and hockey (he was captain of the College 1st XI). In his latter years at St John's he hardly ever missed a day's schooling and blossomed academically. Sitting his exams in December 1940, a year earlier than the other boys in Upper Vb, the sixteen-year-old Endean obtained a Class 1 in the Matriculation Certificate Examinations, a result that is inscribed on an oak-panelled honours board that still hangs in the school. The St John's College Register records that, as well as his matriculation result, Endean had (underlined in red) a 'Group IQ 130'.

Endean stayed on in the sixth form, and for the 1941 Lent term was made both head of Alston House and captain of the College cricket XI. The team he led fielded to a high standard, but the batting relied over-heavily on their skipper – going in at the top of the order, he did not fail in any of the matches, scoring 330 runs with an average of 82.5 (the second best average was 16). In the loss to Jeppe, he carried his bat for 69 in his side's total of 98; and he made 68 in a drawn game against Pretoria. But his highest innings, and most satisfying result, came in a victory against near neighbours and deadly rivals, King Edward's School (KES). In the two-day match starting on 28 February, St John's batted first and, after being 10-2, their captain batted 'confidently and freely' for 143, which included 20 fours. The only other significant contribution was a hard-hitting 35 from Mike Bold of timeless house-match fame. Declaring at 293-8, they bowled their opponents out for 155. Led by Endean, who took two catches and made two stumpings off the bowling of leg-spinner T.K. Wilton (7-54), the team's outstanding fielding drew numerous rounds of applause from the banks of spectators. This appeared to be the beginning of a glittering final two years at St John's, but Endean stunned the school by deciding to leave after only a single term in the sixth form. Alston's declared their sorrow at losing their Head of House, while wishing him 'the best of luck as a "working-man"'.

****

Endean's decision to leave school prematurely seemed strange – the school had expected him to star on the College's rugby, hockey and cricket fields, in addition to preparing for a place at university. But normally prosperous families were finding things hard-going during the early years of the war, on top of which Endean's father had been diagnosed with early-stage Parkinson's disease in 1935. In these worrying circumstances the seventeen-year-old felt he had an obligation to contribute to his family's household finances. With the first-class matriculation result under his belt, he had no trouble in finding a traineeship at a leading Johannesburg accountancy firm. His thorough preparations for the world of work included listing in a notebook (still in the family archive) the buses he would have to take from 1 Kernick Avenue, Melrose North, where the family was now living, to the city's financial centre. But life was not all work and evening classes. He joined the Old Johannians Club (subscription £4.4.0) where he soon made his way into the 1st XIs for cricket and hockey – in the latter team he was a fast and skilful centre-half, representing Johannesburg while still only seventeen. The Old Boys had recently established Linksfield, a new clubhouse and sports ground adjacent to the Royal Johannesburg Golf Club. They opened the ground in 1939 with a cricket match against local rivals Old Edwardians. Batting with only ten men (Ronnie Grieveson was 'absent on military duties'), OJ's lost their last wicket just before close of play, with only nine runs needed to win. The Johannian protested that 'Hitler caused Johannians' defeat.'

In peacetime the OJs 1st XI had played at the top level of Johannesburg Club cricket, but during the war league cricket was suspended, and instead the Old Boys kept the game alive by playing a series of matches against military teams. In one such game, a January 1942 fixture versus a South African Artillery XI, 'the feature of the Old Johannians innings was a finely played 81 by the promising young batsman Endean.' A 1941 team photograph shows a fresh-faced Russell Endean in amongst a group of middle-aged men and one even older – the fifty-eight-year-old St John's College coach, Humphrey Yates. School cricket also continued during the war; and Endean was asked to play for A.P. Walshe's XI both against his old school and at the Wanderers ground, where he top scored with 64 in the defeat of Jeppe School. But, apart from the odd day off, sport was limited to Saturdays and Sundays; during the week he pored over books on company accounting, taxation and business management. And on 4 January 1942, tucked away on an inside page of the *Rand Daily Mail*, was an announcement that, after a less than a year of study, he had passed Sections A & B of the Intermediate Examination of the South African Accountants Society.

Old Johannians
Russell Endean standing on the right

By this time, several former St John's College cricketers had been killed in action, amongst them Squadron Leader C.B. 'Caesar' Hull DFC, an OJ who died flying with the RAF in the Battle of Britain. He earned his DFC flying a Gloster Gladiator – single-handedly shooting down four German aircraft that were machine-gunning troop concentrations. He was described as 'a king among men and one of the finest pilots the RAF had'. Like him Russell Endean was one of scores of young South African men who felt they had a patriotic duty to serve in the forces. The whole of his matriculation class at St John's College volunteered to fight in a conflict 5,000 miles from home, and on his eighteenth birthday Endean followed them – joining the South Africa Artillery (SAA) Regiment. After seven months of intensive training as a gunner (although occasionally he returned home for some cricket with Old Johannians), on 4 January 1943 he left the safety of his family home to go to war.

****

Several wartime photographs of Russell Endean, his face still boyish and slightly chubby, have survived. One sensitive study by Russian émigré photographer Leon Leveson, husband of the leading ANC activist Freda Leveson, perfectly captures the face of a young man nervously contemplating an uncertain future. His first posting was to Egypt where khaki berets, open-necked shirts, long baggy shorts and heavy-duty, highly polished boots were the order of the day.

For his first year, Endean's Armoured Division prepared for future battles by taking part in a series of military exercises. Away from manoeuvres there was time for sport: SAA won an international shooting competition, receiving their trophy from King Farouk; while the division's rugby team suffered a humiliating defeat at the hands of a New Zealand XV. But, over a year after leaving home, 330220 Gunner W.R. Endean (pay, 6/- a day) was still waiting to see action. Writing home, his frustration is evident: 'I'll proudly be able to say that I won the war in the guard room and kitchens.' Another five-page letter to his mother and father written at the beginning of 1944 is bursting with news of a recent leave. He describes the tortuous train journey from Egypt to Palestine, and well versed in Bible stories – St John's College had taught him well – he details visits to the Garden of Gethsemane, the Mount of Olives and 'the Pool of Bethesda – the pool into which Jesus placed the

New recruit, May 1942   *Kitted out for the Middle East, 1943*

lame man, if you remember the story'. He celebrates the spotlessly clean hotel room in Jerusalem, 'the city of peace'; and is pleased not to be pestered by orange-selling Egyptian 'Wogs'. He describes swimming in the Dead Sea, 'You can't sink'; and shopping – he bought 'a fairly compact complete Works of Shakespeare at only 9/-' and 'a little brooch for you Mom – I was quite taken with it.' Other goodies he only looked at: 'I handled some fine cricket bats and hockey sticks – Len Hutton's and Autographs in abundance – real beauties.' Politics reared its horned, but perhaps should have been avoided, head: 'I was involved in a fairly vociferous argument with one of the more communistically inclined members of our party concerning the honesty of the stock exchange.' But his most disarming experience was on the often-precarious dance floor:

> I entered full of confidence. There was an insufficiency of girls so it meant plenty of sitting out. They say fortune favours the brave, but it was otherwise that night. The first time I danced with one of the two attractive girls – they played a none too distinctive waltz. I afterwards found out it was an old-fashioned waltz and I was left badly at the start and cracked up. After standing wondering what to do I felt I must do something, and naturally did not do the right thing. Fortified by a cup of tea I failed in my effort with the other girl – they played another waltz and she tactfully suggested we sat out early on. So that was that.

Summing up his Palestinian adventure, Endean astutely judged the lie of the Holy Land: 'There is of course the big conflict between Arabs and Jews, the Palestine police more or less acting as a buffer.' His heartfelt letter ends: 'The date is 4/1/44. One year ago today I left home. I am not sorry, as on looking back I have had some marvellous experiences and times. They are taking the lights away now so good bye. With love to you both, Russell.'

Early in 1944, the nineteen-year-old soldier did eventually get closer to the action. As a gunner he manned '105 mm. "Priests" and when those wore out, switched to 25 pounder self propelled Sextons.' His regiment was part of the 6th Armoured Division of the South African Artillery that landed at Taranto on the heel of Italy, where they were part of the Allied Forces invasion under the command of Lt-Gen Mark Clark, the handsome young American commander who controversially ordered the bombing of the ancient abbey at Monte Cassino. The advance took them through the city of Caserta where Yorkshire and England left-arm spinner Hedley Verity is buried – he had suffered fatal wounds during the previous year's Allied invasion of Sicily. The retreating German army continued to put up strong resistance to the Allied advance, an obduracy that irritated Gunner Endean:

'Logically it would seem that the Germans have no reasons for continuing, but still they do. Perhaps they are hoping for a stalemate or a split in the Allies, costly hopes.' Restrained by the military censor's blue pencil, this was a rare comment on the war; mostly, and sometimes elegantly, he wrote about the sites he saw and the books he read. In August 1944 he made two visits to Rome, where he was forced to explore the eternal city's splendours on foot, complaining that the taxi drivers, 'getting back to normal, were charging exorbitant prices'. Six months later, along with three other soldiers (all of whom signed the theatre programme), he went to see *Don Giovanni* at the Teatro Reale Dell' Opera di Roma. As well as soaking up culture whenever and wherever he could, he also read widely – Shakespeare, the King James Bible and poetry, particularly Shelley. 'There is a passionate rhythm about his verse. His style reflects his nature, passionate and ecstatic.' Inspired by Shelley's *Ode to Naples*, the young man, almost certainly destined for a future life in the grey world of accountancy, in an October letter to his mother and father, had a stab at describing autumn in Italy, using some colourful Shelleyesque prose:

> I see the green fields and others ploughed, the soil being rich, black and earthy – a fine soil, a soil of which to be proud. Meandering lines of bushes indicate the streams where water flows. Trees are scattered about the slope – the leaves of some are still green, others are tinted with varying shades of yellow, some being all yellow, while oak leaves turn to reddy brown. Fitting into the scene are houses, some white or stone and even a pink one, with their roofs red, and near the houses are haystacks. Westward come the mountains. The slopes of the nearer ones can be seen to be red-brown, beyond they loom distinct against the horizon, their valleys and chasms blue-black, the sun lighting the slopes. Snow still glints from fissures of the highest peak. So the western panorama is one of the magnificent mountain range, the mountains standing distinct and majestic against the blue sky.

By the end of 1944, sporting an impressive Clark Gable moustache, perhaps to lure innocent young Italian girls, the twenty-year-old was at last at the front. Fellow gunner M.L. Wellington – reviving schoolboy rivalries – reported in *The Johannian* that Endean and I 'were on the same gun and managed to form an OJ combine to combat the Old Edwardian influence.' But Wellington goes on with more disturbing news that his fellow gunner was evacuated from the front line suffering from diphtheria, although he 'is now in a convalescent camp near Perugia.'

On May 3, having first accidentally trodden on Lt-Gen Clark's cocker spaniel, General von Senger und Etterlin, Commander of XIV Panzer Corps and speaking in perfect English – he was Oxford-educated, with an English wife – surrendered German land forces to the Allies. The war in Italy was over. Gunner Endean, having recovered completely from his life-threatening illness and by now back with his regiment camping in the shadows of the Alps, penned a final letter home. His sentiments combined calm acceptance with relief: 'I can write without the thought of snipers and mines dimly filtering through my mind. No longer do I keep an ear open in case a shell should arrive.' There is a tinge of regret – he was so near to Venice, a city he longed to visit – but with the arrival of peace, rather than another Italian adventure, his thoughts turned to picking up the pieces in South Africa. He hoped he could 'combine into civilian life the best of what I have learned in the army.' He closed his last wartime letter to his parents with a deeply felt message: 'How pleased and relieved you must feel that it is over – there are no worries now. Let us thank God for bringing peace and for bringing me safely through.'

****

After Endean's regiment had celebrated the European Armistice with a Victory Parade on the motor-racing circuit at Monza on 14th May, there was a tedious nine-month wait before he was discharged, during which time he received a very tempting invitation from Springbok international Matthys 'Boy' Louw to play for the divisional rugby side on a tour of England and the Continent. For a young man always keen for new experiences, this must have been a difficult offer to reject; but he turned it down, deciding instead to get back to Johannesburg and play some cricket before the end of the South African summer. He eventually arrived home, weather-beaten and sporting his six campaign medals: the 1939-45 Star, the Africa Star, the Italy Star, the Defence Medal, the War Medal 1939-45 and the Africa Service Medal. However, for four young men of his school matriculation year, there was no return – along with some ninety other former pupils of St John's College, they had fallen in action. These harsh realities and the brutal experiences of war had transformed Russell from an innocent schoolboy to a hardened young man, happy and grateful to be back home. For the Endean family it was a doubly joyous celebration as elder son Howard, a Flying Officer in RAF Special Reserve, had also come back safely. The first news of Russell's return was a brief piece in the Sporting Gossip column of the *Rand Daily Mail*, reporting that just over a week after his return from the northern hemisphere, and without any practice, he had scored 19 for Old Johannians Cricket Club against Pretoria at Berea Park. It was February and there were only a few more weeks of the season left, but he managed to fit in nine games. In the next match against Wanderers he scored 109 before lunch, in an innings in which he had to pit his wits and technique against a fine spell of bowling by the veteran Test leg-spinner Xenophon Balaskas, who took 6-116. The *Rand Daily Mail*'s headline read: 'ENDEAN PROVES NEW TRANSVAAL CRICKET HOPE'. Club matches in Johannesburg at this time were sprinkled with Test and first-class cricketers. In the fixture against the Wanderers, Bruce Mitchell and Ronnie Grieveson were playing for OJs and their opponents included, as well as Balaskas, past and future South African opening bowlers David Ironside and Geoff Chubb. In the last match of the season OJs had to win to top the Transvaal Sunday League, and thanks in part to Endean's confident, fast-scoring, undefeated 81, his side scored the 271 needed to beat Old Parktonians. The OJCC, captained by Mitchell, finished equal top with Wanderers, and also won the Lionel Phillips Saturday competition. Endean had scored 470 runs in his nine innings, averaging 58.75. Unlike many returning soldiers who found it difficult to adjust to civilian life – for many, even sleeping in a comfortable bed took some getting used to – he seemed to slip effortlessly back into his former way of life. While weekends were spent in cricket whites, from Monday to Friday he was quick to don a grey office suit and resume his career as a trainee accountant. Remarkably, within three months, he had taken and passed Section A of the Final Examination; one more exam and he would be a fully qualified accountant. For the twenty-one year-old, the future looked full of promise both on and off the sports field.

Chapter Two

I Don't Think Endean Would Have Had A Chance

When the de-mobbed Endean returned to South Africa in the autumn of 1946, although a talented rugby forward or full-back (at 5ft 10ins perhaps too small to reach the top level), he chose hockey as his winter sport. Playing for Old Johannians, his outstanding performances as a strong and skilful centre-half were soon being highlighted in the press. 'The game at Linksfield was marked by a magnificent goal by Russell Endean who was in the centre half position,' reported the *Rand Daily Mail*. 'Obtaining the ball on his own 25 yard line, he weaved his way through the opposing defence to score one of the finest goals ever hit in Transvaal hockey.' His talents were quickly recognised and he became a regular member of the Transvaal side playing in the annual Inter-Provincial Hockey Tournament.

In 1948 the Swallows, a combined team from Oxford and Cambridge Universities, visited the Union. They played a series of matches against the provincial teams, losing 3-1 to a Transvaal team captained by a moustached Endean (reviving the Clark Gable look). Also playing for the province at left-inner was Athol Rowan, the South African Test off-spinner who had toured England the previous summer. A sympathetic press attributed the tourists' defeat to an excess of winter heat and hospitality. One other contributing factor for the Swallows going down in this fast-moving game would have been the rarefied air in Johannesburg, a city 5,750 feet above sea level. The visitors finished their tour with a 'Test' match against South Africa. The game was played in Johannesburg on 5 September in front of 10,000 spectators on an immaculately turfed Balfour Park pitch. The home team's players, who were awarded their 'Springbok' green-and-gold colours, came out winners 3-2, thanks to a last-minute goal by Rhodesian centre-forward, Harold Downey. The Swallows fully deserved a draw but offered no excuses and paid tribute to their opponents and in particular to the outstanding work of Endean playing at half-back. 'Time without number this fine player robbed the English international right wing, John Maples, of the ball, and he was always on the spot to thwart dangerous attacking by the Swallows down the centre,' reported Ian Balfour in the *Johannesburg Sunday Express*, 'his covering-up left little to be desired and he fed his wing, Freddie Hilder, with a succession of good passes.' Endean's boundless energy and stamina on the sports field, which he was to show in many performances in years to come, must have been due to some extent to his extraordinarily low pulse rate, said to be somewhere between 40 and 50 beats per minute. A steady heart rate would also have been an advantage

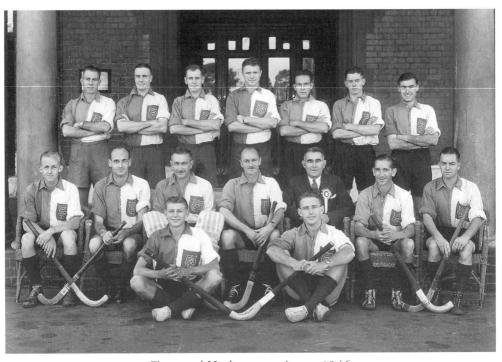

Transvaal Hockey team, August 1946.
Three Springboks cricketers in the back row:
Athol Rowan (far left) Ken Funston (third from right) and Russell Endean (far right)

Endean scores for
Transvaal against
Rhodesia, 1954

during his encounters with various examination boards; Endean had sailed through his school matriculation and preliminary accountancy exams, and in May 1947, aged twenty-three, he passed the final exam that qualified him as a fully fledged accountant.

The next challenge for Russell Endean was to establish himself in the higher ranks of South African cricket. Following his impressive games for Old Johannians, at the end of the 1945/6 season he was picked as a member of the Transvaal provincial squad. And, less than two months after his demobilisation from the SAA, he made his first-class debut at the Ramblers Cricket Club Ground in Bloemfontein against Orange Free State. After OFS had been dismissed for 106 (with veteran leg spinner Balaskas taking 7-48), Endean opened the batting for Transvaal, making 95 and sharing a second-wicket partnership of 135 with Alan Melville (Oxford University, Sussex, Natal, Transvaal and South Africa). Transvaal won this final fixture of the season by an innings and 19 runs, Balaskas finishing with match figures of 10-160. It was an auspicious start for the young Johannesburg accountant but, despite this, the following season he was not a regular selection for the strong Transvaal side, playing in only three games, two of which were Currie Cup matches. He featured in a low-scoring cup match against Eastern Province: batting at number eight he scored an unbeaten 48, and at number nine in the second innings, with his side in need of quick runs before a declaration, he opened his shoulders and scored a rapid 26 not out; Athol Rowan took 11-69 in the Transvaal victory. This was the first-ever game at Ellis Park, the Old Wanderers ground having been demolished to make way for Johannesburg's new railway station. Despite averaging 53 for the province in his first two seasons, he was not picked for Transvaal for another two years, and only once in 1949/50. Even though Endean was competing for a place in a team with a very powerful batting line-up full of Springboks players – in the 1946/7 season Bruce Mitchell (159) and Alan Melville (153) shared a partnership of 299 for Transvaal against Griqualand West – this was a frustrating time for the twenty-six-year-old.

Despite continuing austerity in post-war South Africa – there were still widespread food and fuel shortages – the predominant issue during the country's 1948 election was the segregation of the races. The National Party's commission on apartheid published on 29 March said that: 'The Party undertakes to protect the white character of our towns. The Native in our towns must be regarded as a visitor with no claims to political rights there.' The election result two months later was a turning point in the country's history. The National Party, and its ally the Afrikaner Party, won 79 seats (with only 39.4% of the vote) and ousted Field-Marshal Smuts's governing United Party and its ally, the Labour Party. The National Party, under the leadership of the Dutch Reformed cleric D.F. Malan, was now in a position to implement even harsher segregation laws than those already in force.

Sport, like the rest of South African society, was strictly divided along racial lines, and any concerns that Russell Endean might have about such policies had to be kept to himself if he wanted to play cricket at first-class level. He had been given very few chances for Transvaal in the first four years after the war, but following some outstanding performances for Old Johannians during the early part of the 1950/1 season, and a polished sixty in the province's trial match, he was given a run in the Transvaal side as a wicket-keeper batsman. In the first Currie Cup match of the season at the Salisbury Sports Club, he took six catches in Rhodesia's first innings – the first time this had been achieved in the competition's history; but in his only knock he managed just four in Transvaal's innings victory. He scored 275 runs at 39.28 as well as taking 16 catches and making two stumpings in the six matches he played for Transvaal. His highest score was 99 not out at Newlands made on New Year's Day against Western Province, the young wicket-keeper batsman being left high-and-dry just one short of his maiden first-class century; captain Eric Rowan having declared Transvaal's second innings at close of play with their score at 353-9. He had batted for nearly three hours and, needing to score 20 runs off the last eight ball over of the day to reach his century, he managed a valiant 19. Louis Duffus, the doyenne of South African journalists, lyrically described the day's play for the *Johannesburg Star*: 'The incessant wind agitated the Newlands oaks as Endean, whose flannels are often sprinkled with the grit of stone-walling, poured out all sorts of enterprising strokes from Mrs Hubbard's factory.' Tough as it was on Endean, missing out on his maiden century, the Transvaal declaration could have said to have been fully justified: on the final day they sent down almost 98 overs, and there was only twenty minutes remaining when they finally bowled out WP for 318 (Clive van Ryneveld making 138) – this victory by 146 runs

W.R.
ENDEAN
(SOUTH AFRICA)

contributing significantly to Transvaal eventually becoming the 1950/51 Currie Cup champions. For Endean this was a groundbreaking season. He had finally established himself in the provincial team, and his eye-catching performances with bat and gloves earned him a surprise selection as the first-choice keeper in the South African team to tour to England in 1951. The majority of critics had wanted the experienced Natal stumper Bob Williams, but former Springbok Bob Catterall backed the selectors: 'Endean is the more consistent keeper. He is our best since the late Jock Cameron.'

****

A large crowd gathered at Johannesburg's railway station to wave farewell to the England-bound Transvaal players as they travelled south to meet their fellow tourists in Cape Town. One story of a meeting with the Prime Minister in the 'Mother City' just before the tour party set sail, told by Clive van Ryneveld in his autobiography *20th Century All-rounder*, highlights the extent to which cricket at this time was very much an English-speaking game in South Africa: 'Dr Malan was asked to meet us which he willingly did over a cup of tea [at the House of Assembly]. In his friendly speech he expressed the hope that we had enjoyed our tour in South Africa. He thought we were a visiting English team.'

Veteran batsman Dudley Nourse captained the 15 men – all weekend cricketers – who sailed to England on the *Arundel Castle*. Apart from the skipper, there were two others in their forties: vice-captain and experienced opening batsman Eric Rowan, and the un-capped medium-pacer Geoff Chubb. There were also two thirty-year-olds: batsman Jack Cheetham, and Shropshire-born leg-spinner Percy Mansell. The remaining ten players were all in their early-to-middle twenties: three batsmen, George Fullerton, Jackie McGlew and Roy McLean; two spinners, Athol Rowan and Norman 'Tufty' Mann; two fast bowlers, Cuan McCarthy and Michael Melle; one all-rounder, the Oxford double-blue and England centre-three-quarter Clive van Ryneveld; plus two wicket-keeper batsmen, John Waite and Russell Endean. Hugh Tayfield, who had taken 27 wickets at 16.14 for Natal in the domestic season, was very unlucky to be omitted from the original squad, but was called up later when Athol Rowan's dicky knee seemed unlikely to last the summer. The manager of the team was Sidney Pegler DSO, a former Springbok leg-spinner who had taken a record 189 wickets on the 1912 tour. The tourist's baggage master and scorer was the ubiquitous Australian, W.H. 'Bill' Ferguson. For their 192 days away from home, the team of amateurs were compensated for loss of earnings with a £500 payment, as well as their expenses, travelling and hotel accommodation being paid for.

The Britain that greeted the Springboks when the *Arundel Castle* docked at Southampton on 20 April 1951 was a country only gradually emerging from six years of grinding austerity. Under Clement Attlee – a cricket devotee who followed the county scores on a tickertape machine installed at 10 Downing Street – the Labour government, despite huge wartime debts, had achieved a great deal. Key industries such as steel, coal and the railways were nationalised, the National Health Service and a cradle-to-grave welfare state were established, the education system was totally transformed and there was full employment. But as their boat train approached London, the South Africans may well have been taken aback by the many overgrown bomb sites and the general drabness of the people and the country. However, leaving Waterloo for their West

End headquarters, their spirits might have been lifted a little by catching a glimpse of a group of recently completed buildings sitting on the south bank of the Thames. The Festival Hall, the Dome of Discovery and the Skylon were amongst modernist structures that were part of the forthcoming Festival of Britain, a shiny, ground-breaking exhibition that would act as a symbol of hope for a nation looking towards the second half of the twentieth century.

Having settled into the luxury of the Park Lane Hotel on Piccadilly, the team strolled along to nearby Simpson's, where they were fitted with their green-and-gold-striped Springbok blazers. They then went across the Thames to Borough High Street where Stuart Surridge supplied the whole team with their top-quality bats for the tour. On 23 April the team took the short journey to Lord's for their first net practice in warm spring sunshine. Michael Melford of the *Daily Telegraph* noted that 'the tall fair-haired C.N. McCarthy' bowled at a pace 'that is not often exceeded in this country today.' The *Daily Herald*'s Charles Bray was even more expansive, reporting that McCarthy has 'a fine action with a tremendous follow-through, and is probably the fastest bowler in the world.' Always keen to unearth a tourist with a connection to the mother country, *The Times* discovered that Russell Endean (described as a 'protégé of Bruce Mitchell') had a mother from Yorkshire and a Cornish father who had recently been in England celebrating his retirement. On hearing of their son's selection when they arrived back in Johannesburg, the proud parents immediately booked another trip to England to see their boy playing for South Africa. On 28 May Endean was in the South African team to play in a one-day match at Luton against the Club Cricket Conference. Not a ball was bowled so both teams were able to watch the FA Cup Final between Newcastle United and Blackpool (one of the few football matches shown live on television) in which Geordie hero Jackie Milburn fired home two second-half goals to give the Tyneside team a comfortable 2-0 win.

By the time of South Africa's first county fixture, dreadful spring weather had set in. The tourists were greeted at the County Ground in Worcester by cold wind, rain, sleet, thunder and lightning. Endean, batting at number seven was clean bowled by the medium-pacer George Chesterton for just 4 in his first first-class innings in England. The weather was just as icy for the next fixture against Yorkshire at Bradford Park Avenue. 'Even Capt. Scott and his gallant band would not have ventured out in the conditions,' remembered Endean in a 1975 article on Fred Trueman for the Wombwell Cricket Lovers' Society. 'However if any spectators did survive, they will recall seeing an outstanding bowling performance by Fred which all but earned Yorkshire an innings victory. Our last pair just held out, with Trueman's figures of 15-6-19-5 telling the story.' Endean, in this match batting at number three, had failed again with scores of 5 and 14.

Endean and Eric Rowan at the start of the 1951 tour

Only six Springboks had previous experience of English conditions, and photographs of these early games show the tourists swathed in layers of sweaters, as they struggled with the grim weather and unfamiliar soft pitches. They won only one of their first ten games (against Glamorgan, by an innings), the rest finishing as draws. Endean as first-choice keeper played in most of them, averaging 25.3, with his best two scores against Surrey in the final game before the first Test. He made 37 in the first innings and, although he started with a delightful late cut for four, it was a case of almost exclusively dour defence during his two-and-a-half-hour stay at the crease. In the second innings he made a breezy 72, highlighted by some powerful pulls to the boundary. But, despite this late show of batting form at the Oval, the selectors felt that his keeping had been so leaden-footed that they chose instead the twenty-one-year-old John Waite (who a week earlier had made 128 against Essex) to open the batting and keep wicket in the opening Test at Trent Bridge.

Freddie Brown and Dudley Nourse at the toss, First Test, Trent Bridge

This proved a shrewd selection, the debutant making 76 in a first-innings score of 493 for 9 declared – a near two-day effort that Alex Bannister in the *Daily Mail* called 'just one big yawn'. And A.J. Turner's verdict in the *Nottingham Journal* was that the 'South Africans went to sleep on a Trent Bridge featherbed.' The visitors' total was dominated by a courageous nine-hour innings of 208 by captain Dudley Nourse, batting throughout his stay with a recently pinned thumb, broken while fielding a hard drive from Tom Graveney in an earlier match against Gloucestershire. England replied with 419 (Simpson 137, Compton 112); and although South Africa only made 121 in their second innings (Bedser, bowling almost unplayable leg-cutters, taking 6-37), the tourists went on to win a tight game by 71 runs, with Athol Rowan (5-68) and 'Tufty' Mann (4-24) spinning England out for 114 on a worn fifth-day pitch. South Africa's victory was only their second in England following their win at Lord's in 1935.

In the next county game following the Test match, the tourists hung on against Northants for yet another draw, having followed on 214 behind the county's total of 426. In the South Africans' first innings, batting at number three, Russell Endean made a two-hour 57. He failed in the second innings making just four, before being dismissed for the second time by George Tribe, the Australian left-arm spinner playing his first game for the Midlands county. It was left to stand-in captain Eric Rowan, who batted for 6 hours 40 minutes on the final day, scoring 202 not out, to fend off any danger of defeat for the tourists. Buoyed by their success at Trent Bridge, South Africa then travelled hopefully to Lord's for the second Test; but, after restricting England to 311, heavy overnight rain produced ideal bowling conditions for the second and third days' play, and South Africa were unceremoniously bowled out for 115, and, following on, 211. The lanky Bolton-born off-spinner Roy Tattersall was the main destroyer with match figures of 12 for 101. Captain Nourse and vice-captain Eric Rowan bowled the four overs needed for Len Hutton and Jack Ikin to knock off the 16 runs required for England's ten-wicket victory.

Russell Endean in his only innings before the third Test was out for a duck in the tourists' innings of 499 against Combined Services – a team that, in the days of National Service, included Jim Parks, Brian Close, Fred Titmus and Alan Moss. Endean was not picked against Yorkshire at Bramall Lane, Sheffield. In another drawn game, in which each side only batted once (S.A. 454-8 dec., Yorks. 579), there were centuries for South Africa's Clive van Ryneveld (150) and Yorkshire's openers Len Hutton (156) and Frank Lowson (115). After this stalemate, South Africa crossed the Pennines for the third Test at Old Trafford where they were again resoundingly beaten, this time by nine wickets. In a rain-affected match, it was the thirty-three-year-old Alec Bedser who demolished the tourists with figures of 12-112. The South Africans could consider themselves slightly unlucky not to hang on for a draw, as on the final day Hutton (98 not out) scored the winning run only minutes before the heavens opened once again.

After the series of high-intensity matches, the tourists travelled north to Glasgow where they played a rain-affected drawn game against Scotland at the Hamilton Crescent ground (scene of the first ever Scotland versus England football match played in 1872). The team then crossed the Irish Sea where they completed two comfortable victories against Ireland, the first in Belfast and the second on Dublin's grand Trinity College ground. Following weeks of basic meals in England where there was still rationing of meat and other foods, the South Africans cricketers were promised 'juicy steaks' when they reached the fair city. 'Within an hour of arrival,' wrote C.O. Medworth in *Noursemen in England*, his entertaining book about the tour, 'faces were aglow with anticipation, silence reigned, excepting for explanations of delight as large steaks appeared.' Endean, although fortified by some prime Irish beef, was still unable to come to terms with the many soft pitches and the turning ball: in six innings between 11 and 24 July he scored a meagre 56 runs. Despite this poor form, he did not sulk or grow depressed during his five months in England; as he had done during his army days, he made the most of what the tour had to offer away from the cricket field. Pursuing his love of music, he made frequent visits to the Royal Opera House, Covent Garden. He saw Victoria de Los Angeles singing the lead in *Manon*; Kirsten Flagstad and Sigurd Bjorling in *Tristan and Isolde*; *Aida* starring Joan Hammond; and at Glyndebourne, Birgit Nilsson as the Veronese beauty in Mozart's *Idomendo*. The whole Springbok team went to St James's Theatre to see Laurence Olivier as Caesar and Antony and Vivien Leigh as Cleopatra in the sell-out theatrical event of the summer, in which the two stars, on alternate nights, performed Shaw's and Shakespeare's versions of the Egyptian queen's story.

After their early defeat at the Lord's Test, the South Africans also had time for a trip to SW19 to watch the first day of the Wimbledon Championships, (the singles winners: Dick Savitt and Doris Hart, both Americans). Not all their organised visits were as enjoyable and relaxing – most towns and cities still had thriving local industries that they wanted to show off to the tourists, and the team were duty bound to show their faces at many official functions. These included visits to Viyella's Nottingham factory, where each player was given a welcome gift of two cricket shirts. During the Leicestershire game, the team went to Byford & Co's Blackbird Mills, where photographs taken for the *Leicester Mercury* show a group of smartly-suited young men taking a commendable interest in the manufacture of socks. Following their six-wicket victory at Grace Road, the tourists travelled to Leeds for the fourth

The Joy of Socks – a visit to Byfords & Co

Test. Despite being the first-choice keeper for the tour, Endean was in such poor form that there was no question of John Waite losing his place as the Springbok wicketkeeper; the Old Johannian was still waiting for his Test debut.

Dudley Nourse duly called correctly for the third time in four Test matches and chose to bat on a perfect strip. The Springbok batsmen made full use of the ideal conditions, batting for an hour short of two days. In their total of 538, Eric Rowan (who often batted without a box or gloves) made 236, breaking the record for a South African in Tests, previously held by his captain who had made 231 against Australia in 1935. 'He might have been born in Yorkshire,' recalled Len Hutton. 'I doubt if there's been a harder cricketer come out of South Africa than Eric Rowan.' The third day started in blissfully warm summer weather, with thirty thousand Yorkshire folk packed into Headingley to see two of their own open for England. In demeanour, mannerisms and build, the twenty-six-year-old, Bradford-born Frank Lowson, with his shirt sleeves rolled up to an inch below the elbow and sporting a dark-blue England cap, was almost indistinguishable from his hero and mentor Leonard Hutton. A tentative Lowson appeared to get an edge to a McCarthy lifter in the opening over but, when the exultant appeal was turned down, the unbelieving Waite hurled the ball towards mid-on. 'A catch it was off the inside edge of the bat,' declared Natal journalist C.O.

Medworth, who nevertheless was prepared to forgive the official. 'Where is the umpire who has not erred? Heaven forbid that robots should control our games.' Lowson made the most of his reprieve, scoring an elegant 57 before being beautifully caught by the bespectacled Mansell in Athol Rowan's leg trap. This brought Old Carthusian Peter May to the crease to join Hutton for his first Test innings. By close of play he had joined the fairly select band that have scored a century on debut, ending on 110 not out, with England 325 for 3. Excited by the appearance of this tall, fresh-faced Cambridge undergraduate, EW Swanton in the *Daily Telegraph* reported that his batting 'had a steadfast calmness and concentration of purpose remarkable in a young man of 21.'

Sunday was not a do-as-you-please rest day for the tourists; they were taken on yet another organised trip, this time by a special coach to York, where they were shown round the Minster by the Dean of York, the very Rev. Eric Milner-White. They would however have been back at their hotel in time to watch the 8.15 BBC broadcast of *The Final Test*, a play about the dying-of-the-light of Sam Palmer, an ageing England cricketer. *The Times* complimented both the production, and the script by Terence Rattigan (who had been opening the batting for Harrow versus Eton at Lord's in 1929): 'His humour is gay and impudent.' There was also praise for Patrick Barr who 'made Palmer's simplicity touching without being absurd.' A photograph in *The Listener* of Barr wearing an England blazer gives him a look a great deal more convincing as the veteran batsman than the rotund, middle-aged Jack Warner who played Sam Palmer in the 1954 feature film version of the play. Back at Headingley on Monday morning, the South Africans spent over half of the fourth day in the field, England finally being dismissed for 505 (May 138, Hutton 100). Rowan and Waite put on 87 before close of play, but heavy early-morning storms meant no play on the final day, which denied the tourists any chance of forcing a win on a fifth-day pitch.

Four further matches were fitted in before the final Test. The tourists criss-crossed the country: beating Somerset, drawing with Warwickshire and Sussex and then, in front of a huge sun-drenched holiday crowd at St Helen's, Swansea, playing in an exciting, low-scoring game against Glamorgan. Captain Nourse put the home side in to bat and soon after lunch they were dismissed for 111 (Mansell 5-37, A. Rowan 4-54). Endean opened the South African innings with John Waite and made 13 before being caught by Allan Watkins in Len Muncer's leg trap. He was the only batsman in the top seven to reach double figures, on an almost unplayable pitch; the Springboks were 36-7 at tea, eventually finishing level on first innings with 111, mainly thanks to two tail-end contributions from Athol Rowan (49) and Mansell (21), Hampstead-born off spinner Muncer taking 7 for 45. Welsh rugby

The South African XI, The Oval, 1951
Back (left to right): WR Endean, PNF Mansell, CB van Ryneveld, CN McCarthy, MG Melle, RA McLean   Front: JE Cheetham, AMB Rowan, AD Nourse, EAB Rowan, GWA Chubb

international and Glamorgan captain Wilf Wooller top-scored with 46 in his side's second innings total of 147 (Rowan 4-42, Mansell 4-73). Amazingly, the young replacement off-break bowler Hugh Tayfield had not bowled a single ball in either innings on a pitch made for spinners. The South African openers Waite and Endean (neither of whom kept wicket in this match) put on an untroubled 54 for the first wicket, and the match looked all over; but once Endean was out for a well-played 38 (his highest score for two months), in the next three-quarters-of-an-hour the rest of the side collapsed to 83 all out, Durham-born off-spinner Jim McConnan taking 6-27, including a hat-trick. Glamorgan were the first county to beat the tourists, the Welsh team winning in front of their fervent supporters by 64 runs. Wooller was chaired off the field with the crowd cheering and singing *Sospan Fach* and *Land of our Fathers* – a scene reminiscent of a Wales rugby international victory.

****

Preparations for the final Test were not going smoothly for the South Africans – a match that, if they could force a victory, would level the series. 'Tufty'

Mann had a strained back but more worryingly was complaining of pains in his lower abdomen. His replacement was the twenty-one-year-old Transvaal fast bowler Michael Melle. John Waite had damaged his right forefinger and would not be risked so Endean, who earlier in the week had gone to Lewes Races with the Duke of Norfolk, was selected to play at the Oval. After a frustrating summer in which he had shown poor form both as a keeper and batsman, at the age of twenty-seven he would gain his first cap and become a Springbok double-international.

Nourse won his fourth toss of the series and chose to bat. Under a limpid blue sky in front of 27,907 spectators, the new cap was asked to open the batting with vice-captain Eric Rowan. The pair were not unduly stretched by the opening attack of Alec Bedser and Derek Shackleton, and the two medium-pacers were soon replaced by a contrasting pair of off-spinners, Jim Laker and Roy Tattersall. They immediately found the wicket responsive to spin, with Laker in particular frequently turning the ball past the forward stroke and rapping both batsmen on the front pad. Rather than this first-morning traction being a cause for concern, from some there was a warm welcome for the strip that the groundsman had produced. 'Bert Lock said that he had prepared this pitch for a three-day and not a five-day match,' claimed Edgar Turner in the *Daily Mirror*. 'By his preparation of this wicket on which the ball turned from a very early hour, [he] has restored some sanity to Test cricket.' Not surprisingly, with so much spin, both batsmen were concentrating on defence, and were soon being slow-handclapped and jeered at for what the restless Oval crowd saw as tedious play. Endean did manage a few attacking shots: he off-drove Tattersall for four and later stroked a leg-spinner from England captain Freddie Brown past cover point for another boundary. But only a few minutes before lunch, with the score at 66, Endean was dismissed. He was given out caught Brown off the bowling Laker but, although he quietly accepted the verdict of umpire Frank Chester, at the time there did seem some doubt in the minds of the catcher and the wicketkeeper, Don Brennan. Having caught the ball at backward short leg, Brown immediately flicked the ball back to Brennan who whipped off the bails while the batsman was scrambling back to his crease; a half-hearted appeal for a run out was made by Laker, but immediately up went Chester's finger at the bowler's end having judged that the ball had hit both bat and pad. Endean had to go, having made a hard-fought 31 in his first Test innings. During the afternoon session, once Eric Rowan was out for 55, South Africa's middle order was swept aside (despite 41 from Athol Rowan), and they finished with a disappointing total of 202. Laker on his home patch had bowled 37 overs and taken 4-64. In the evening session England immediately lost Lowson for nought, neatly gloved two-handed low down the leg side by Endean off Melle's second ball in Test cricket in England. After this early alarm, Hutton and Peter May seemed to have taken England safely through to stumps but with the many contented spectators starting to make their way home, Hutton playing back to an Athol Rowan off-break, missed and was plumb lbw for 28. With England 51-2 at close of play, South Africa were still in with a chance of squaring the series.

In contrast to the first day there was a slight drizzle in the air when the players arrived at the Oval on Friday morning for the second day's play. There was a twenty-minute delay before the first ball was bowled by medium-pacer Geoff Chubb, and it was obvious after a few overs that the rain had taken some spite out of the wicket – Athol Rowan was not getting nearly as much purchase as he had on day one. After forty minutes, and 28 hard-earned runs had been garnered, the persevering Chubb found some late in-swing to pluck out May's middle stump. This brought in England football international Willie Watson to join Arsenal winger Denis Compton. The pair batted serenely through to lunch with the score at 111-3, after which some outstanding South African fielding pinned back England. First to go was Watson, thrown out by McCarthy with a direct hit at the bowler's end after the Yorkshire left-hander had been sent back by a hesitating Compton. He had made 31 and England were 128 for 4. Next to go was Brown, caught spectacularly by van Ryneveld throwing himself forward from Rowan's leg trap. Another fine two-handed catch by Endean, diving full length in front of first slip off the bowling of the hostile Melle, dispatched Bedser. The

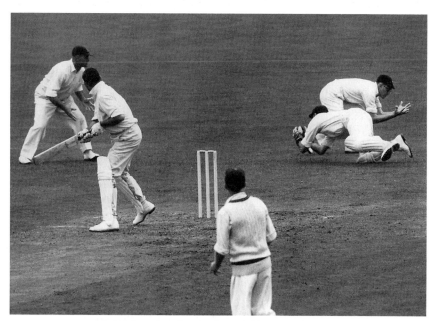

Endean catches Bedser, Fifth Test, 1951

37

debutant quick bowler then cleaned up the tail, finishing with remarkable figures of 10-6-9-4. England were all out for 194, with only Compton showing any resistance after Watson was dismissed; the Middlesex matinee-idol had batted with uncharacteristic watchfulness for 220 minutes, making 73 before being last out, bowled by McCarthy.

South Africa were not having much luck with the conditions – late-afternoon sunshine had dried out the pitch by the time the tourists started their second innings. Endean was first to go, playing well forward to Bedser he allowed the ball to strike his front pad, thinking he was outside the line, but umpire Dai Davies disagreed, and he was leg-before for 7. Laker then had van Ryneveld trapped in front for 5, which brought in Dudley Nourse. Aware that it was the forty-two-year-old South African skipper's last appearance in England, the Surrey crowd gave him a standing ovation. But batting with the still-not-healed thumb, he was desperately out of touch and, attempting to cut Laker, he played on for just 4. South Africa lost no more wickets, finishing the day on 68 for 3, but not before Hutton had shelled out two catches offered by Eric Rowan. On a wearing pitch the match was still delicately balanced.

18 August, the third day of the Test, clashed with the start of the English football season. Earlier in the month there had been a number of pre-season friendlies, including Aston Villa versus West Bromwich Albion at the Mitchell & Butler's Ground – AVFC scored 104 (Tommy Thompson 42, Fred Richardson 3-37, Jim Sanders 2-15) and beat WBA who made 94 (Ronnie Allen scoring 15) by ten runs. Among this opening Saturday's football league fixtures there were three First Division afternoon games in London to attract fans away from the Oval: Arsenal were playing Huddersfield Town at Highbury; at The Valley Charlton Athletic were at home to Burnley; and it was Fulham versus Preston North End at Craven Cottage. Despite full houses at these three juicy north-south encounters, 25,000 Ovalites had turned up under a sunny South London sky to see Eric Rowan and Jack Cheetham resume the South African innings. After a cautious opening half hour, Rowan was the first to depart; aiming across the line towards the open spaces in Laker's leg-side field, he missed and was lbw for 45. Although, like Endean, his front foot had been well down the wicket, this did not deterred umpire Davies from unhesitatingly raising his finger.

For the whole of this third day's play the South Africans had allowed the distinguished photographer Jack Esten access to the inner sanctum of their dressing room. Esten had made his name taking dramatic pictures of the Second World War, and later would take many memorable photographs of iconic Hollywood stars including Marilyn Monroe, Audrey Hepburn and Jack Nicholson. During his day with the Springboks, he came up with some intimate pictures of tense moments during the South African's second innings.

Endean lbw Bedser 7

One black-and-white study of Endean with his head in his hands captures the disappointment of his side's disastrous collapse, during which they lost seven wickets for seventy, finishing with a meagre second innings total of 154. On his home ground, Jim Laker, plugging away tirelessly with his elegant, over-the-top action, finished with figures of 28-5-6-55 (10-109 in the match). But the result was still in doubt. England's target of 163 would not be such a stroll if Athol Rowan, in particular, could dominate on the bowler-friendly wicket.

England's captain Freddie Brown had ordered Bert Lock's heaviest roller to be used between innings, and openers Hutton and Lowson scored 50 runs in forty minutes while McCarthy and Melle were bowling on the deadened pitch. But once the effects of the roller had worn off, Rowan began to elicit some spin, and one ball that lifted more than anticipated led to the singular dismissal of Len Hutton. Attempting a sweep, he miscued, and the ball looped up – according to conflicting reports – off either the top edge of the bat or his glove. As Endean scrambled round from behind the stumps, Hutton swatted the ball away with the back of his bat, preventing the keeper, who by now was on his knees, from making the catch. Immediately Nourse and Eric Rowan, close by in the leg trap, appealed. Umpires Dai Davies and Frank Chester – who was standing at point to avoid looking into the setting sun – exchanged glances, before Davies gave the Yorkshire opener out. While a puzzled Hutton was slowly departing, Chester trotted across to the pavilion and shouted up to the scorers that the decision was: 'Obstructing the field' – the first such dismissal in Test history.

The press leapt on the incident. 'HUTTON GIVEN OUT IN TEST MATCH SENSATION' was the banner headline in the 'Late Night Final' edition of the *Evening Standard*. Views about the decision were mixed. 'He clearly baulked wicketkeeper Endean from making the catch,' wrote Douglas Jardine in the *Sunday Express* and 'equally clearly this was Hutton's intention. Umpire Dai Davies gave the only possible decision.' E.W. Swanton in the *Daily Telegraph* was not quite so sure: 'Hutton apparently did not realise that he had snicked the ball. Thus it could be said that the obstruction was not literally wilful as the law demands, and there would seem to be a case for a rephrasing which took away any implication of unfairness.' Fellow wicketkeeper in the match Godfrey Evans was in Endean's camp: I feel [he] had good reason to appeal and the decision was quite fair.' But the victim did not agree, and Hutton was quoted in the next day's *News of the World* as saying: 'I'm in a daze. The ball hit my glove ran up my arm and I used my bat as it was about to hit me in the face. There was certainly no deliberate obstruction. It is said I stopped a possible catch. I don't think Endean would have had a chance.' However, many years later the by now knighted Yorkshireman conceded that 'the [umpires'] decision was quite correct.'

After Hutton's dismissal, off the next ball Rowan had May triumphantly taken by his brother Eric at forward short leg. 'For the last time,' John Arlott would write in *The Cricketer* 'the scoreboard showed "caught E Rowan bowled A Rowan."' Van Ryneveld then caught Lowson at short leg off the same bowler and England were struggling.' England still needed 79 to win and there were certainly worries in the England dressing room, but these were quelled by some middle-aged slogging from skipper Brown who, with a great deal of fortune, made a rapid forty. He later confessed that he had downed a large whisky-and-soda before going into bat. The final stroke in the dramatic day came from England's bowling hero Jim Laker, who quietly turned Rowan to fine-leg for three. England had won by four wickets. There was considerable praise for Bert Lock's wicket: 'A pitch which, while safe and reasonably lasting, gave the spinners scope from the word "go",' wrote Ian Peebles, who summed up by declaring that it had been 'one of the best matches of the year'.

The general consensus was that despite losing the series 3-1, South Africa had fought well during a particularly wet, chilly and inhospitable summer. Five senior members of the team were never to play for their country again. Dudley Nourse's broken finger did not recover and he was forced to retire. The thirty-year-old Athol Rowan, with a worsening knee injury picked up while serving in Abyssinia, was also forced to quit after the trip to England. The forty-year-old Geoff Chubb – the most successful Springbok bowler of the summer (21 Test wickets at 27.47) – started and finished his international career on the 1951 tour. On his return home, Eric Rowan was asked to retire gracefully by the South African cricket authorities, which he refused to do, and was never picked for his country again. Although a reason was never given, the suspicion was that it was his protest in the match against Lancashire that cooked his goose. Along with Waite, he had taken part in a sit-down by the side of the pitch after being slow-handclapped by the Old Trafford crowd. Eventually play resumed, and soon afterwards Rowan was dismissed for a stubborn, three-hour 66. As the exhausted opener made his way back up the pavilion steps he was subjected to some fruity abuse from a Lancashire member, to which Rowan was quick to reply in kind (he said he also 'stamped on the gentleman's foot'). After a tense, late-night meeting in the team's hotel, South Africa's manager Sid Pegler decided his behaviour unacceptable and proposed sending him home. But persuaded by captain Nourse, he eventually decided on a different course of action, instead reading out a fulsome apology on the player's behalf. 'Eric was wrong to sit down on the Old Trafford pitch, yet his "crime" was never worthy of the punishment meted out to him,' was the verdict of baggage-master Bill Ferguson in his autobiography *Mr Cricket*. And he quoted the 1952 *Wisden*: 'The Springboks taking home a record profit of £17,500, instead of meeting with financial catastrophe, was due solely to one man, Eric Alfred Burchell Rowan'.

The saddest end to a career was that of Norman 'Tufty' Mann. Having been joined by his wife Daphne who had travelled from Transvaal to be with her ailing husband, he stayed in London for three months after the tour for two major abdominal operations. Despite further surgery when he returned to Johannesburg, the doctors could not save him, and he died of cancer in Hillbrow on 31 July 1952, aged 31.

There were several more fixtures after the Test at the Oval including the end-of-season festival games at Hastings and Scarborough plus a trip across the North Sea to play two matches against the Netherlands in Haarlem. For the traditional line-up in front of the Scarborough pavilion, Russell Endean sported a new moustache above a wan smile. But the fresh growth brought no change of fortune, his tour ended as it had begun: in the last first-class match of the season, against T.N. Pearce's XI, he scored 1 and 0. Both his batting (527 runs at 18.17) and his wicketkeeping had fallen well below expectations. He had found it difficult to cope with the varied pace and bounce of the wickets in the dank, cheerless English summer. Charles Fortune's verdict was that 'Endean failed to justify the tremendous reputation foisted on him by the Transvaal press and public.' During the thirteen-day voyage back to South Africa on the *Winchester Castle*, the twenty-seven-year-old had plenty of time to ponder whether his days as a Springbok cricketer were over.

Chapter Three

No Hopers

Former Test captains and the majority of the South African press were of one mind: the 1952/3 tours to Australia and New Zealand should not go ahead. Seven of the most experienced and successful cricketers from the 1951 tour were not available, and the remaining untried and inexperienced players would be no match for an Australian team that the previous season had handed out a 4-1 thrashing to the unofficial world champions, the West Indies – a team that contained, as well as the legendary three Ws (Everton Weekes, Frank Worrell and Clyde Walcott), the two little spin bowlers, Ramadhin and Valentine. The Australian Board of Control, aware of the apparent weakness of the South African team, would only agree to the tour as long as the South African Cricket Association bore all the expenses of the tour. To its credit, and despite all the opposition, the SACA decided to take the risk.

Among the tour party was Russell Endean. After his disastrous time in England, picking the twenty-eight-year-old seemed to be a high-risk selection. Nevertheless, a recuperating season of domestic cricket for Old Johannians and Transvaal, plus a good performance in the end-of-season trial match, earned him a berth on the boat. He had missed some early-season cricket because, now working for the United Building Society, he had been away on a branch audit in Port Elizabeth. However, on New Year's Day 1952, batting at number six and making up for lost time, he scored 140 in a Currie Cup match at Ellis Park against Eastern Province. This was his first first-class century, nearly six years after his debut. Then on the third day of the trial match (the first two days were washed out), opening the batting for J.E. Cheetham's XI against D.J. McGlew's XI, he top-scored with 41. This carefully constructed innings on a difficult pitch, together with his season's average of 55.16, was enough for the selectors to give him the nod. The rest of the fifteen-man party was: thirty-two-year-old Western Province batsman Jack Cheetham (highest Test score 54), who would captain the side; he along with Jackie McGlew, Percy Mansell, Roy McLean, Michael Melle, John Waite and Hugh Tayfield had all been to England in 1951, though none had had a particularly impressive tour. The remainder of Cheetham's men comprised opening bowler Eddie Fuller; batsmen Ken Funston, Gerald Innes and Eric Norton; and all-rounders Headley Keith, Anton Murray and John Watkins. The tourists again employed the popular Bill Ferguson as the team's baggage master and scorer; and the manager was the forty-two-year-old former Test batsman, Ken Viljoen.

Prior to the team's departure, Viljoen contacted Danie Craven, former Springbok rugby player and coach, and by then Professor of Physical Education at Stellenbosch University. Craven issued each player with a list of instructions for general fitness as well as specific exercises for batsmen and bowlers. He stressed that running was important for stamina, broken up by sprinting and turning; for footwork, plenty of skipping; and for strengthening the abdomen: 'Back-lying and slowly raising both feet, opening them as you do so, closing them as you lower them.' And, what sounds like a particularly tough exercise: 'Feet fixed, trunk raising (slowly) and lowering it so the back of the head touches the floor first.' Craven recommended that batsmen stretch their arms, shoulders and hamstrings before they go out to bat saying that 'It is not so much the warming up which matters but the loosening up of important muscles.' For bowlers he felt both loosening and warming up was essential, 'as it has been proved that some bowlers have to be taken off just when the maximum performance ability has been reached because they had wasted their first two or three overs warming up.' On diet, he felt that a poorly functioning stomach created spots before the eyes, so 'batting starts with the stomach and if some are prone to liverishness, the cause will have to be ascertained and eliminated.' Craven was ahead of his time in recommending fish, fruit and salad, but thought 'meats and lots of it are most essential.' And, music to some cricketers' ears, he thought it 'sometimes worse to be a tee-totaller than a moderate drinker.'

1952/53 tour of Australia
The players in the all-important tour committee: McGlew, Cheetham & Endean

Conscious of the label of 'no-hopers', the South African players were keen to prove the doubters wrong, each one preparing thoroughly before they set sail. Watkins and Keith had themselves filmed to eliminate faults; McGlew and McLean practised their hook-shots against young tyros who flung down high-speed short stuff on concrete pitches; while Gerald Innes and Jack Cheetham pounded round the sports fields of Cape Town's Rondebosch School. Cheetham had had considerable doubts about going on the tour when his wife Norma became ill, but the hospital specialists thought it would be far worse for her if he turned down the trip. As for Russell Endean, to prepare for Australia, he had managed in September to get time off to go on a three-week tour to Kenya with the Durban Crickets. Endean was part of an inner circle that included Cheetham, McGlew and Viljoen who had been in constant touch during the weeks before the tour, discussing match tactics and the strengths and weaknesses of both their own team and their opponents.

Standing on the Cape Town quayside, Jack Cheetham, addressed the assembled press and one of the smallest groups of well-wishers ever to bid farewell to a South African cricket team. He announced that, despite all the criticism, he was convinced that they would 'do well' and 'mould into a happy side with confidence in our ability to play cricket as it should be played.' Once the *Dominion Monarch* had rounded the Cape and was steaming due east across the Indian Ocean, the team got down to the serious business of preparing for the tour. The players, incorporating Craven's exercises, worked for an hour each morning with the ship's physical training instructor. Also before lunch, there were meetings between the 'senior management' of Viljoen, Cheetham, McGlew and Endean, who discussed with individual players their place in the batting order and best fielding positions; and for the bowlers, their preferred field placings. There was also time for relaxation as well as the traditional deck games. The players built up team spirit by holding a team meeting at 7.45 each morning, during which fines were handed out for such serious crimes as being late for meetings (2s. 6d.), being unshaven (1s.), missing ship's church services (1s. 6d.) and 'rustling' or pinching each others' girl friends (2s. 6d.). At the ship's end-of-voyage concert, the players performed, to great acclaim from passengers and crew, a skit on commercial radio. The stars were Russell Endean as 'Snarls Scorpion, the Cricket Commentator'; Jack Cheetham as 'Chit Chatterbox, the Friendly Announcer'; with Roy McLean, Ken Funston and John Waite as the close harmony group the 'Almond Icing Trio'.

****

The team landed at Freemantle on 13 October 1952 and immediately travelled to Perth to set up a base and get straight down to practice with a series of routines that had been carefully planned during the voyage. Initially

44

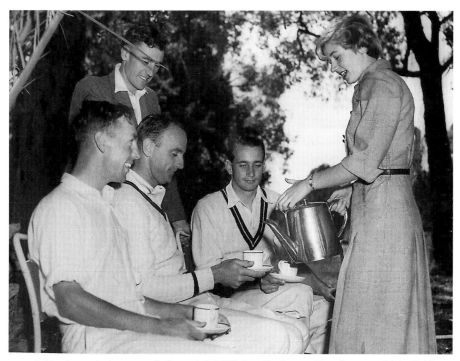

A Perth tea lady serves (left to right) Waite, Endean, Cheetham and Tayfield

there was a concentration on fielding and then personalised practice for the batsmen, providing them with specific bowlers to improve any identified weaknesses. The quick bowlers were given new balls to see how much swing they could generate in unfamiliar Australian conditions.

A cartoon by Jock Deyden in the *Natal Daily News* at the time of the tourists' arrival, highlighted one of the wider concerns of the Australian public. A kangaroo custom inspector is pictured examining a South African cricket bag and asking the question: 'Any atom bombs in this lot?', to which the Springbok manager replies 'I'll tell you at the end of the tour.'

The locals had been blaming a spell of bad weather on Britain's first atom bomb, exploded on 3 October at the Monte Bello Islands off the coast of Western Australia. While in London the *Daily Mirror* was celebrating with that old mantra that 'Britain is GREAT BRITAIN again', Australians were concerned about not only the meteorological effects but also reports that hundreds of thousands of dead turtles had been found on the islands' beaches. It was not until 1991 that the British government – admitting that not only turtles died but that aboriginal people living on the mainland had illnesses relating to radiation exposure – reluctantly agreed to pay $45 million in compensation to the Australian government.

The atomic fall-out did not stop the sun shining on 25 October for the Springboks' first match of the tour – an overwhelming victory in a one-day game against Northam and Country Districts. The opening first-class fixture against Western Australia turned out to be a mind-numbing draw. The South Africans batted for nearly two days, scoring 427. Endean was tried as an opener, going in first with McGlew (182); he made a confident 34 in two hours at the crease. Hugh Tayfield opened his tour with a gentle spell of 48.2-14-98-5 in WA's only innings total of 306.

The tourists' 1325-mile journey from Perth to South Australia across the Nullarbor Desert was made with Trans Australia Airlines, a relief to all those who could remember the hot and dusty four-day train journey of previous tours. The weather was cold and wet when the South Africans arrived in Adelaide, and the Oval was too cut-up after a recent Aussie Rules fixture for practice to be possible. Endean was rested for the match against South Australia that started on 31 October, a drawn game in which only stubborn resistance by Cheetham and Keith staved off defeat after the tourists had had to follow on. The relatively poor start to the tour brought out what the *Rand Daily Mail* described as 'another of Australia's inky attacks on a cricket touring team ... a continuance of the post-war "knocking" campaign.' Adelaide's Kevin Hogan in *The Sun* thought the visiting pace bowlers 'barely up to Test match standard', while former football star turned distinguished sports writer Percy Beames in the *Melbourne Age* demanded that 'for the good of all, McCarthy and Rowan should be sent out.' This comment displayed a lack of knowledge of South African cricket politics: Eric Rowan's sit-down protest on the 1951 tour to England had condemned him to the outer darkness, and Cuan McCarthy had drawn his brief first-class career to a halt after he was no-balled for throwing by umpire Paddy Corrall while playing for Cambridge University in 1952. Frank Chester, a fine all-rounder with Worcestershire who had turned to umpiring after losing his right arm at Salonika in the First World War and was by now England's most revered umpire, had wanted to no-ball South Africa's fast bowler in the first 1951 Test at Trent Bridge, convinced that he threw. But Chester first 'sought the prior support of Sir Pelham Warner' who, according to Tim Quelch in *Bent Arms and Dodgy Wickets*, 'refused to support him, cautioning: "These people are our guests."' Chester, worried about losing his job as a Test umpire, drew back from calling the young Springbok bowler.

Undaunted by this early wave of criticism but encouraged by the legendary former Australian bowler Bill O'Reilly, who thought they were a splendid fielding side with not a 'glass arm' among them and that it was far too early to write them off, the team travelled optimistically on the overnight train to Melbourne. Their comfortable wide-gauge Victorian State Railways' train

Endean catches Loxton in Tayfield's leg trap, Victoria v South Africa

Spirit of Progress impressed the captain Cheetham – in his book about the tour *Caught By The Springbok*, the transport obsessive described his overnight accommodation: 'The "Roumette" is sufficiently large for one person to sit in in comfort, and by merely pushing a switch, the built-in bed folds down, another switch brings a wash-hand basin down, and yet another controls a concealed toilet.' After net practice at a damp Melbourne Cricket Ground, the team went to a show starring the British entertainer and devoted Fulham FC supporter Tommy Trinder. The Cockney comedian with his catch phrase 'You lucky people!' told the audience – with a nod to the tourists – that, across London, Charlton Athletic had on their books five South Africans, adding that two of them (Stuart Leary and Sid O'Linn) were also first-class cricketers.

The Springboks' match against Victoria was watched on the first day by 10,000 spectators – a fair crowd that nevertheless looked lost in the 100,000-capacity MCG. The weather was overcast and humid, and the South Africans struggled all game against the Victorian seam bowlers; but thanks to a downpour on the last afternoon, the visitors managed to hang on for a draw (Endean making 15 and 35). Off-spinner Hugh Tayfield took 7-71 including a hat-trick in Victoria's second innings. This result did not staunch the criticism coming from the Australian press; nor did the loss in the next game at the Sydney Cricket Ground to the Sheffield Shield champions, New South Wales – a team led by Keith Miller that included Ray Lindwall, Arthur Morris, Sid Barnes, Alan Davidson, Richie Benaud and seventeen-year-old Ian Craig, the 'new young Bradman'. The five-star batting performance for the Springboks was delivered by Russell Endean: as well as scores of 77 and 95, he took three astonishing catches while fielding at straight silly-mid-on to Tayfield. One of these sent the N.S.W. captain on his way. '[Endean] dived at a terrific drive from Miller and rolled across the pitch with the ball clenched in his hand,' wrote former Aussie leg spinner Arthur Mailey in Sydney's *Daily Telegraph*. 'The crowd stood and cheered, despite the fact that that this catch had robbed them of their cricket idol.' Endean's outstanding all-round performance helped to persuade some of the doubters that he had the class to be an international cricketer. *Sydney Sun* journalist Dick Whittington was one who had changed his mind: 'Two weeks ago I would not have considered Endean as a Test prospect. Now he should be the first choice.' Such opinions were reinforced in the next match against Queensland. After almost two days in the field – during which wicket-keeper Don Tallon, coming in at number eight, scored 133 in the home side's 540, Endean batted for over seven hours for an unbeaten 181 in the visitors' first innings score of 362; and when the South Africans followed on, his 87 did much to save the game. 'Endean's splendid batting,' declared Bill O'Reilly, 'has been an inspiring morale-building tonic for the young South African side in the coming Test.' Not withstanding such encouragement, the Australian press was still not convinced that the South Africans, with their weakness in fast bowling and lack of big-game players, were worthy opponents for the home side. In fact one critic even demanded that the series be reduced from five to three matches.

****

The first Test started on 5 December at Brisbane's unsophisticated Woolloongabba ground in temperatures close to 100 degrees. Jack Cheetham, having lost the toss, led South Africa out in front of a sparse crowd – many fans were boycotting the match because of the lack of any Queensland players in the Australian team. The locals were particularly hostile towards keeper Gil Langley, who had been preferred to their own Don Tallon – they cheered the visitors and threw insults at the home team's players. When Australia's captain came in, he was greeted with: 'You're too old, Hassett; you need a bath chair.' On a perfect batting pitch the Springboks restricted the Aussies to a first innings total of 280, left-hander Neil Harvey making a dazzling 109, his fifth century against South Africa in six Tests. The below-par Australia total was thanks mainly to the bowling of the twenty-two-year-old Michael Melle (6-60), the pace man who had been written off by the press. The other factor that kept the score down was the outstanding run-saving, ground fielding and catching of Cheetham's athletic young team, whose average age was 26. The South African score of 221 in reply was disappointing – eight players were in double figures, but the highest was 39 – while Endean's recent form deserted him, as he scratched around for 14 before being caught at the wicket off leg spinner Doug Ring (6-72). Cheetham, writing after the tour, was unhappy with some 'not out' decisions in Australia's second innings, which allowed them to reach 277 (Melle, with another three wickets, finished with match figures of 9-166). Chasing 337, the South Africans put up a good fight; but on a wearing pitch and facing a fine spell of fast bowling from Ray Lindwall who took 5-60, including Endean for 12, lbw on the back foot to a very quick skidder, the visitors fell 97 runs short of achieving an unlikely victory. But the general opinion, even amongst the hostile home press, was that the young Springbok side had put up a strong challenge in the opening encounter.

The day after the first Test, the team flew to Sydney for a drawn game against an Australian XI; Endean kept wicket rustily but made amends with an uncharacteristically skittish innings of 45 in an opening stand of 67. The team – less Endean, who had gone fishing – then moved on to Ballarat for a fixture against a Victoria Country XI. For some of the tourists the highlight of the visit to this former gold-mining town was an atmospheric candle-lit carol concert at St John's, Soldier's Hill. On arriving in Melbourne, following two days of net practice, music-lover Russell Endean along with some of the team had an evening out at His Majesty's Theatre to see *South Pacific* ('Some Enchanted Evening', 'There is Nothing Like a Dame'). The uncompromisingly progressive message on mixed-marriage and racism in Rodgers and Hammerstein's pioneering smash-hit musical would not have been lost on the young South Africans in the audience.

After an early-morning Christmas Eve walk through the cool, aromatic Fitzroy Gardens, Jack Cheetham and his players entered the steamy and oppressive atmosphere of the Melbourne Cricket Ground for the first day of the second Test, knowing that the Australian press were still not giving the visitors much hope of a victory – Tom Goodman was not alone in seeing the match mainly as a trial for the Australians' 1953 tour to England. South African manager Ken Viljoen must have been particularly happy to see the large number of dapperly-dressed spectators queuing at the many entrances to the MCG, given that so far the gates for the early matches had been poor and, since the Springbok were having to self-fund their tour, it was vital that the crowds picked up for the remainder of the fixtures. Skipper Cheetham, who had declared an unchanged XI for the second Test, was delighted to win the toss but the morning session turned out to be calamitous for the Springbok top-order. Waite was caught at first slip off Miller's first ball; Endean batting at three, attempting to cut Lindwall, was caught at second-slip by Richie Benaud; and Funston – after struggling against some fine sustained swing bowling from the two thirty-somethings – eventually fell to an expertly disguised slower ball from Miller. Wickets continued to fall regularly either side of lunch before the tall schoolteacher Anton Murray raised the score with an aggressive 57 to a barely respectable 227. Kevin Hogan's verdict was that Keith Miller and Ray Lindwall – Australia's greatest match-winning cricketers since the war – had 'virtually already won the second Test against South Africa.'

To try and prove the hard-nosed newspapermen wrong, the Springboks first had to get through a tedious Christmas Day. The phone lines home to loved ones were down; and the festive dinner, prepared and served by chefs and waitresses who would no doubt rather have been elsewhere, took several hours to get through. Such a damp squib of a day, however, did not deter the South Africans, and on their return to the MCG on Boxing Day they fought back with great spirit to dismiss the Australians for 243. With two of their quicks injured, the slow bowlers Tayfield and Mansell did the bulk of the work, the off-spinner taking 6-84 in a four-hour spell. The bowlers were again backed up by some outstanding catching and fielding. As well as Endean's celebrated one-handed boundary catch to dismiss Miller, Tayfield's caught-and-bowled to remove Arthur Morris would live long in the memory of those who witnessed it – the left-handed opener drove the off spinner hard and high at silly point where a leaping Cheetham, with hands above his head, managed to parry the ball towards mid-off. Tayfield turned and ran several yards before flinging himself full-length to catch the ball two-handed and only inches from the ground. In the words of Percy Beames, it was an 'amazing catch – a tribute to quick reflexes and ability to regain balance with remarkable agility.' All day waves of applause rang round the MCG, the large holiday crowd captivated by a mesmeric display of fielding from the athletic young Springbok team.

South Africa, 6-0 at the close of play, resumed their second innings on day three in front of an expectant 36,000 Saturday crowd, the impartial amongst them hoping to see the visitors put up a strong showing. McGlew fell early, stumped by Langley as he charged Ring, with the score on 23. This brought Endean to the crease. First with Waite, who made 62, he put on 111 for the second wicket; there then followed further valuable partnerships – 62 hard-fought runs with Funston (26); and then in the last 55 minutes of play, a partnership of 75 with McLean, who in a typically dashing innings laid into the wilting Aussie attack, hitting six boundaries in his 42. South Africa were 267-4 at the close of the third day, with Endean undefeated on 115. Recognising the quality of this gutsy, day-long innings, the huge, sun-drenched Melbourne crowd gave the Springboks' number three a prolonged ovation as he made his way to the cool of the MCG's Victorian pavilion. This

Morris, caught and bowled Tayfield, Melbourne, 26 December 1952
In the first picture Cheetham leaps and parries the ball
In the second Tayfield dives full length to catch it

chanceless and undefeated century that had put his side in the box seat was acclaimed by Bill O'Reilly, who was not always an easy man to please: 'The purposeful way in which he set about his responsible job was an inspiring example to his team mates.'

Before the South Africans could continue their second innings they had to kick their heels during the rest day on Sunday – Russell Endean spent the time writing letters home, listening to music on his radio, and in the afternoon walking with Jack Cheetham in the city's verdant Botanical Gardens. On Monday morning there was another 30,000 crowd waiting to greet the two men who walked out to resume South Africa's innings – because of the two rest days, this was now almost a week since the match had started. The middle order of Cheetham and Watkins did not contribute a great deal, and it was left to the tail to support Endean as he guided his team to a total of 388. The Transvaal man, whose previous highest Test score was 31, had batted for seven and a half hours for 162 not out, "I kept my head down reasonably well,' Endean recollected disarmingly, 'and the runs just seemed to come.' Although his chanceless innings had not been sprinkled with classical eye-catching strokes – most of his nine boundaries, hit with his well-taped bat,

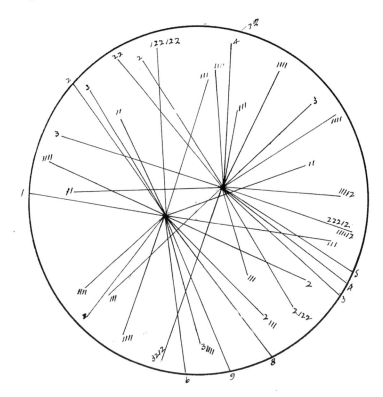

The scoring wheel for Endean's 162

had come from thumping sweeps, square-cuts and hooks – the fourth-day Melbourne crowd's generous applause for the demure Endean was prolonged and heartfelt; they recognised it as a potentially a match-winning innings against a full-strength attack at the peak of its powers.

Set 373 to win, Australia, after hard-fought resistance, were finally dismissed for 290 on the final afternoon of the match. The handsome, dark-haired, six-footer, Hugh Tayfield, who had taken 7-81 (13-165 in the match), was cheered off the field by the Melbournites, happy to support the underdogs who had beaten Australia for the first time in forty-two years. Although the twenty-four-year-old off-spinner's marathon contribution had been immense, Ralph Barker's verdict in *Ten Great Innings* commands respect: 'Historically the game belongs to Russell Endean. He had followed his catch of the century with a century of character.'

****

The whole mood in Australia had changed; a cartoon in next day's *Melbourne Age* depicting a rampant springbok astride a flattened kangaroo said it all. Rather than the South African Tests being just fixture-fodder – trial matches

for the 1953 tour to England – there was now a rubber to be saved. The press corps, instead of running down the tourists, was now attacking the home side's weaknesses: for P.J. Millard in the *Sydney Morning Herald*, the Australians had been 'humbled' and they now had 'selection problems' that needed to be sorted out before the New Year Test at Sydney.

There were celebrations all over South Africa after the unexpected Test victory – among the team's many congratulations from back home were telegrams from the Governor General, Dr G.E. Jensen, and the Prime

Minister Dr D.F. Malan. Russell Endean – 'South Africa's most eligible bachelor' – received a delightful picture-postcard of two young women enjoying New Year's Eve celebrations in Johannesburg, on the back of which they had written: 'With lots of love from your South African girlfriends & wishing you all the luck in the world – we're eagerly awaiting your next big score. Cynthia & Fi.'

'Eagerly awaiting your next big score'

Early on the morning after the Test, the team flew to Sydney where they booked into their Coogee Beach hotel before some brief practice at the SCG. Starting on 1 January 1953, their four-day game against New South Wales was a tough fixture immediately following the second Test, and skipper Keith Miller was not planning to give the visitors an easy ride. The state was at full strength, and the Springboks hung on for a draw only thanks to rain on the final day. The highlight of the game, in which Miller twice dismissed the in-form Endean for 27 and 59, was an undefeated 213 by Ian Craig. Despite this double-century by the seventeen-year-old prodigy, Australia,

Practice at Sydney before the 3rd Test

like South Africa, went into the third Test, which started on 9 January, with an unchanged team. The locals disapproved – one Hillite shouting out 'You only beat Craig in one thing, Hassett, and that's years'.

The veteran Aussie captain lost the toss and was not surprised that Cheetham chose to bat on the rock-hard, but perfect SCG pitch. The South Africans never came to terms with the relentless fast bowling of Lindwall and Miller who unsettled the Springboks with occasional menacing short-pitched deliveries (there was an unofficial agreement between the teams to restrict the number of bumpers), and the visitors were dismissed just before the close of play on the first day for a well-below-par 173 (Endean 18). Australia made far better use of the true pitch, racking up 441 over the next day and a half, as the twenty-four-year-old left-hander Neil Harvey thrilled the 30,000 Saturday crowd with an array of powerful cuts and drives in his consummately assured innings of 190 made in a minute over six hours. South Africa made a slightly better fist of their second innings, managing 232 (Endean 71) but nevertheless losing comprehensively by an innings and 38 runs.

****

Between the third and fourth Tests there was a week-long trip to Hobart for the tourists – minus Anton Murray, who had stayed behind in Sydney for emergency appendicitis surgery. As well as two overwhelming innings victories against Tasmania, there was time for a fishing expedition to the Shannon River; and to be guests of Governor-General Sir Ronald Cross and Lady Cross for morning tea at the grandiose Government House. After their relaxing stay on the luxuriant island, the South Africans flew the 720 miles to Adelaide where they would attempt the serious business of trying to level the series. The temperature was way up in the 90s when the team arrived in South Australia's capital, so they were relieved to be staying at the cooler, coastal resort of Glenelg. There were two days of preparation before the start of the fourth Test: on the first, the forty-four-year-old, and still dapper, Sir Don Bradman had a session in the nets with the South Africans; and after the second day's practice, the team strolled across from the Adelaide Oval to watch the state tennis championships, where among those playing were the Americans Vic Seixas and Maureen (Little Mo) Connolly. The players were so taken with the dynamic five-foot-five-inch-tall Californian teenager – in 1953 she would become the first woman to hold all four Grand Slam singles titles in the same calendar year – that they invited her to be their guest at the forthcoming Test.

On a pitch that was bound to wear considerably on days four and five, the toss was vital. It went Australia's way, and over the next two sweltering days

Don Bradman (padded up) has a net with the Springboks, Adelaide 1953

– Jackie McGlew remembers 'scraping the flies off our foreheads' – the home side posted a massive 530 (Hassett 163, McDonald 154). South Africa's first-innings total of 387 (Funston 92, Watkins 76, Endean 56) enabled the visitors just to avoid the follow-on; but after a quick-fire century from Harvey, before he was superbly caught by Endean one-handed at point off a full-blooded cut, Australia set the Springboks 377 in 257 minutes. The visitors had no chance of reaching this distant total; but thanks partly to injuries to both Lindwall and Miller, they were able to hang on for a scrambled draw, with Endean batting for 125 minutes in a plucky rearguard innings of 17 before, with a quarter of an hour left, he was clean bowled by, of all people, Neil Harvey – one of the little Victorian's only three Test wickets. The draw meant that, much to the surprise of the hard-nosed Australian press, the series was still in the balance. The final act of the drama was to be played out a week later in the cauldron that was the MCG.

Before that decider there was a tough game against a full-strength Victoria side that would finish only two days before the start of the fifth Test. Although this relentless list of fixtures throughout the tour made it hard going for the players, it generated essential income to help balance the books. By the time it came to this stage of the tour, the Springbok manager Ken Viljoen could rest a little easier as costs had been covered – there would be money to bank when he returned home. The feature of the drawn match against Victoria was a century in each innings by Natal's left-handed all-rounder Headley Keith, which earned him a first Test cap.

There were two debutants for Australia: all-rounder Ron Archer; and Ian Craig, the player the public had been wanting to see in the team for most of the season. The home side were severely weakened by the absence of Lindwall and Miller, who had both pulled up at Adelaide. Hassett won the toss and, despite heavy overnight rain and a wet outfield, elected to bat. South Africa did no more than stay in the game on the first day, Australia finishing on 243-2, Morris being run out for 99. The surprisingly competitive cricket played by the tourists throughout the summer had ensured a sizeable attendance for this final Test – on the second day there was a huge Saturday crowd of over 47,000 in the MCG (gate receipts £5,858 17s 1d), most of whom were keen to see the young Sydney chemist's assistant play his first Test innings. They did not have long to wait – captain Hassett was soon out and Craig came in with the score at 269-4; at 17 years and 239 days, he became (and still is) the youngest player to play for Australia. In a partnership of 148 with Neil Harvey, he contributed a stylish and untroubled 56 (five boundaries in his first 26 runs). But the day mainly belonged to his effervescent left-handed partner who once again tore into the Springboks' attack, making 205 in Australia's first-innings total of 520. In what was left of the day South Africa made 48-1, losing Endean, caught behind by Langley off the bowling of Bill Johnston for 18, having been pushed up to open in the absence of the injured McGlew. At the end of the second day of the six-day Test, Tom Goodman gave his prediction in the *Sydney Morning Herald*: 'Australia cannot lose the match. The only question now is whether South Africa can fight out a draw.'

South Africa did put up a good fight over the next day and a half, all the top order contributing to the final total of 435; and in what remained of day four, they reduced Australia to 89-3, a lead for the home side of 174. The next day started cool with drizzle in the Melbourne air. Cheetham decided to attack from the start, crowding the remaining Australians with a ring of close fielders. The tactic worked superbly – six of the seven remaining wickets fell to catches by close-in fielders (Watkins and Endean taking three each). The home side were bowled out for 209, leaving the South Africans needing 295 for an improbable victory. Waite and Endean started the chase at 3.30 pm, putting on 42 before Waite fell to the veteran Geff Noblet for 18. The pitch was now showing more and more signs of wear with occasional balls keeping very low; but no further wickets fell, and at the close the Springboks were 94-1, with Endean undefeated on 57, having batted with typical determination for two and a half hours. Tension was high in the South African dressing room at the start of the sixth and final day of the final Test – another 201 runs and they would, against all the odds, level the series. In front of over 12,000 spectators, Endean started confidently, and with John Watkins took the total to 124 before he was comprehensively yorked by Johnston bowling with the new ball. He had made 70, and in the words of his skipper: 'He had played a dominant innings, in keeping with his great displays throughout the tour.'

Runs now came steadily either side of lunch; but, with the fall of the fourth wicket at 191, the whole tempo of the game changed – as without any trace of nerves, Roy McLean, after being dropped first ball at mid-wicket by Arthur Morris (who failed to hang on to a full-blooded pull shot), proceeded to lay into the Australian attack. He scored 76 in 80 minutes in a partnership of 106 with debutant Headley Keith, who finished 40 not out. South Africa had won a resounding victory by six wickets, squaring the five-match series and answering their critics in full. Telegrams of congratulation from South Africa were soon flooding into the tourists' dressing room; and former Springbok captain Alan Melville, expressing the views of many back home, was quoted as saying: 'I didn't give them a hope of even squaring the series. But I was wrong.' In London *The Times* acclaimed South Africa's victory as their 'greatest triumph'. In Johannesburg Mr and Mrs Endean received a letter from the Secretary of the Old Johannian Club (Ladies' Section), which read: 'we have followed his performance and the team's with great eagerness, excitement and pleasure … Both you and South Africa can be truly proud of Russell.' Meanwhile, back in Melbourne, an Australian, Bryan O'Brien, who had backed the Springboks at odds of 3 to 1, threw a party for the team at Claridges Night Club: a black-and-white snap from the evening shows a collection of smartly dressed players, drinking wine and surrounded by well-wishers, hangers-on and glamorous women – the spoils of victory.

****

Claridges Night Club: Endean, middle back; John Waite, front left

Although the MCG victory was undoubtedly the climax of the tour, it would be still another two months before the tourists could celebrate with their family and friends. For the rest of the trip the players could travel, first in a state of intense elation and then, as the euphoria wore off, play the remaining matches with the relaxed confidence of a team that had proved itself against the best. The day after the Test, the tourists travelled to Adelaide to play a drawn game against South Australia (Endean 126 runs for once out), followed by an easy victory against a Country XI at Port Lincoln. A photograph taken during this game in one of the many Endean family scrapbooks precisely captures the mood of the players: captioned 'A Trip round the Harbour', it shows two young women in summer dresses standing on the deck of a cabin cruiser, amorously encircled by Roy McLean in brief swimming trunks; Russell Endean for once without a tie and – hanging on to the rigging – the blonde-haired bowling hero of the final Test, Eddie Fuller (8-140 in the match).

Next on the tourists' relentless itinerary was a seven-and-a-half-hour journey aboard a Tasman Empire Airways' flying boat to New Zealand. There they played five fixtures during their four-week stay, two of which were Test matches. South Africa won the first, at Wellington's Basin Reserve, by an innings, as New Zealand, whose line-up included the familiar names of Bert Sutcliffe and John Reid, were dismissed in each innings for 172. In the Springboks' total of 524, opener Jackie McGlew, in his first knock for a month, batted for 8 hours 54 minutes, compiling his highest Test score of 255 not out, at the time the highest by a South African in Test cricket; Anton Murray, fully recovered from the removal of his appendix and batting at number eight, scored 109, his maiden (and only) Test century; while Endean, back down the order at number five, made a fluent 41. In the second, drawn Test at Eden Park, Auckland (ground three shillings, Grandstand season ticket one guinea), Endean made 116 and 47 not out. This match ended with some rowdy behaviour by the locals after Cheetham refused to give the Kiwis a sporting declaration. There was little time for relaxation in the Dominion, but on the Sunday of the second Test the players were flown in two rickety bi-planes to the thermal springs at Rotorua; and while in Auckland, Russell Endean visited St Paul's Church where there is a stained-glass window dedicated to his cousin, Trooper Arthur Stanley Endean, who was killed at Gallipoli in the First World War. At the end of the stay in New Zealand there was a gruelling flight back to Perth before the voyage home; waiting for the Shaw Savill Line Q.S.M.V. *Dominion Monarch* to arrive in Freemantle, the Springboks played a final game – an emphatic innings victory against Western Australia.

The team that arrived back in Cape Town on 13 April were greeted to a man as South African sporting champions; but a picture in the next day's *Cape Times* of Hugh Tayfield and Russell Endean reading letters and cards of congratulation was an indication of whom the press thought were the players who had done most to bring about the unexpected drawn series against the unofficial world champions. In the five Tests the twenty-four-year-old Tayfield had averaged 58 eight ball overs per game, finishing with 30 wickets at 28.10 – eleven more than any other bowler in the series. Endean's tour figures were equally impressive: in the Tests he was South Africa's leading batsman with the most runs and the best average, 438 at 48.66; as he was in all first-class matches with 1,281 at 53.37. He also led the way with most catches (ahead of wicketkeeper Waite) with nine in the Tests and 24 in the first-class matches. The quiet and unassuming man, who five and a half months earlier had left Johannesburg as one of a team of no-hopers, returned to South Africa a national hero, having at twenty-eight come of age as a Test cricketer.

Interlude

Reporting on the 1952/3 Melbourne Test, journalist R.S. Whittington, almost as a throwaway, described Russell Endean's innings as 'endless'. This sobriquet was to stick. There were no cricketers in his immediate family, but from his earliest days his father, a regular lawn green bowler, had taken him to the Old Johannians' Sports Club, where he had the opportunity to watch many fine cricketers, especially the textbook stylist, Bruce Mitchell. And it was this great South African batsman who helped him the most, and to whom Endean was to look up to – in a letter to the *Daily Telegraph* on the death of Mitchell in 1995 he called him 'my boyhood model and hero, when I grew up it was my privilege to open the innings with him.' The young Russell copied his mentor's stance, back-lift, some of his scoring shots and his general calm demeanour at the crease. Endean's preparation before each ball had certain quirky idiosyncrasies that were much written about while he was playing. The great Australian cricket writer Ray Robinson neatly captured Endean's set up: 'This Transvaal accountant stands upright awaiting the bowler with his bat lifted halfway up his shins, as if he is afraid the bottom might stick to the ground. As the ball comes he gives the bat a hurried touchdown between his feet and stumps. While this is going on his feet are twitching and gradually spreading apart.' This exact routine was still in evidence in some home video footage of Endean (still wearing his green Springbok's cap) playing in a club match aged 52.

The up-and-down lifting of the bat was uncommon enough in 1953 for it also to be commented on by Bill O'Reilly who noted that Endean 'lifted his bat up as soon as the bowler starts his approach.' This in modern terminology would be described as a trigger-movement – it allowed him to move into his shots, with even forward-defensive strokes often played slightly on the move. Once the ball had hit the middle of what has been described as a bat as wide as a cowcatcher on the front of a train, there was no flourish, no posing: the manner of the stroke reflected the nature of an undemonstrative but nevertheless supremely self-confident and strong-willed man. Whether facing the speed and hostility of fast men like Miller and Tyson; such masters of swing as Lindwall and Trueman; or top spinners of the class of Benaud and Laker, his sharp cricket brain, legendary defensive technique, and powers of calm concentration enabled him to develop a method of blunting the world's best bowlers. During the early matches of the 1952/3 tour in Australia it had been noticeable that Endean was struggling against leg-spinners such as Doug Ring – there were very few wrist-spinners in South Africa in the 1950s – but he quickly worked out that by using his feet he was able to neutralise the spin, a method which for the rest of the season helped him play many long innings and make a sackful of runs. As well as the many singles he accumulated through good placement and speed off the mark, the four attacking shots that brought him the majority of his runs – elegantly illustrated by scorer Bill Ferguson's immaculate run charts of Endean's centuries at Melbourne and Auckland – were the square-cut, the hook, the sweep and the square cover-drive. Opponents and team-mates speak of how, even with a packed off-side cordon, he could thread the ball between the cover fielders, to the frustration of opposing bowlers and captains. 'He had the ability to drive off the front foot past point by opening the bat more than was common in our day,' recalls Clive van Ryneveld in 2016 'as there was seldom if ever a fielder on the boundary between cover and point, as there often is today. It was a very effective stroke, bringing him many boundaries.' His sweep, played with the back leg dropped to the ground, was in the style of Wally Hammond, rather than Denis Compton's more upright sweep. Played with steely forearms honed on the hockey field, Endean's other productive scoring shots were a rasping hook off his eyebrows, and a vicious square-cut – a wonderful example captured on a 1958 black-and-white South African newsreel film that shows him masterfully creaming a wide short ball from Australian quickie Ian Meckiff square to the boundary.

EW Swanton did Endean a disservice when in the *Daily Telegraph* he described him as 'a batsman with ambitions no more flamboyant than his back-lift which is barely perceptible.' The construction of an Endean innings was entirely based on the state of the game and the needs of his side. His chanceless, seven-and-half-hour innings at Melbourne in 1953 was played with a caution that was vital to set up a big enough total for the eventual victory. In his match-winning score of 162 there were only nine boundaries – one hook, backward-of-square; four sweeps square on the leg-side; and four cuts behind square-cover. Sixty-nine of his runs came in singles, many from dabs towards third man; in addition there were five all-run threes, and twenty-one twos. This was the great strength of Endean, he was a team-player who, in the best interests of the side, was prepared both to play whatever role was required; and to bat in any position – his three Test centuries were scored from numbers three, five and six in the order, and he occupied every position from one to eight for South Africa during his Test career.

Endean had two other strings to his bow. From his schooldays he had developed into a sound and reliable wicketkeeper but, after being picked as the first-choice keeper for South Africa's 1951 England tour, he was forced to surrender his position to the brilliant young keeper-batsman, John Waite. This turned out to be fortunate for the Springboks as it resulted in Endean transforming himself into one of the greatest fielders the game has ever seen. The technique he used for taking catches was adapted from his days

as a keeper: he presented his open palms together and slightly away from his body, creating a cup that looked as big as a baseball mitt. This proved to be an almost cast-iron method for taking catches, whether they came gently or like a rocket. Of course, it was not always possible to get two hands to the ball – as well as the famous one-handed catch against the railings at the MCG, there were any number of close-in leg trap and slip catches off the bowling of the likes of Hugh Tayfield and Trevor Goddard. Although his boundary catch at Melbourne is the one most often written about – *Wisden Cricketer* in 2004 rated it as number three in the 'XI Best Outfield Catches' – Endean himself considered his catch to dismiss Peter May at Johannesburg in 1957 to be his best. May, with exquisite timing, had driven fast bowler Heine off his toes at waist-height towards square leg, where Endean, making yards to his left, leapt in front of the umpire and plucked the ball out of the air before thudding to earth. Contemporary newsreel film failed, as it so often did, to

Endean's catching technique: Morris ct Endean b Fuller, Adelaide 1953

capture the catch, but shows seconds later the astonished reaction of May, Heine and the South African fielders to the heart-stopping nature of the dismissal. Needless to say Endean was the calmest man on the field as his team-mates rushed to congratulate him. Former Springbok Bob Catterall, a fine fielder himself, said it was the greatest catch he had ever seen. This piece of fielding was no one-off – he took many of these match-turning catches throughout his Test career, and there was a consensus amongst journalists that he was the outstanding close-fielder of his generation. When in 1953 two Australian cricket writers, R.S. Whittington and Percy Millard, were invited to compile a list of the best cricketers in various categories, both chose Russell Endean as the world's supreme in-fielder.

As a batsman Endean would never shake off the 'Endless' tag, but when the occasion demanded it, he was able to up the tempo and play crowd-pleasing knocks as well as his more usual defensive innings. His career statistics reflected his value as a dependable performer in all weathers: for South Africa he made 1,630 runs at 33.95. But it was Endean's fielding, and particularly his close-to-the-wicket catching that placed him in the top echelons of Test cricketers. Playing for the Springboks, he took 38 outfield catches in 28 matches, averaging 0.76 per innings, a ratio that puts him in the all-time top ten in Test cricket.

Chapter Four

The Vilcheet Plan

In his April 1953 article 'Back To Their Desks and Benches', assessing the recently returned South African team, Charles Fortune highlights two players: Endean ('completely the stoic') and Tayfield ('ebullient and aflame') – who would, he claimed, go without argument into any World XI. But despite this newfound fame, for Russell Endean life very quickly returned to mundane normality. Still living in his parents' Johannesburg house, from Monday to Friday the chartered accountant travelled into his city-centre desk where he number-crunched for the United Building Society. At weekends in the Highveld's ideal climate, it was the outdoor life of cricket in the summer and hockey during the winter. Having turned twenty-nine in May he was still unmarried, a status that won him the title in the press of 'The Most Eligible Bachelor in South Africa.' He had not as yet swept a young lady off her feet – had not yet been bowled over by an ardent Johannesburg beauty.

The South African Cricket Association, as surprised as everybody by the performance of the team in Australia, was canny enough to try to learn from and to bottle some of the secrets of the team's success. Endean was one of the inner circle – Ken Viljoen, Jack Cheetham and Jackie McGlew were the others – who were sent letters from Mr Jack Meyer, Chairman of the SACA, asking them to detail how they had achieved their triumph. Particularly he wanted to pass on to future Springbok teams how they had developed such good team spirit and consistently high levels of fielding (Viljoen called it the 'Vilcheet Plan', an intensive regime of daily fielding practice). Meyer finished his letter to Endean graciously: 'The Board and I appreciate what you four have done for the game in our country … It certainly gave me the greatest thrill of my life.'

Next up for the South African team was a five-match series in the 1953/4 season against New Zealand. Because of the tour, the Currie Cup competition was cancelled and replaced by a series of friendly matches. In one of these games Endean, taking over from Eric Rowan, captained Transvaal for the first time, leading his side to a ten-wicket victory over Border. The Springboks for their part enjoyed a convincing 4-0 win against the Kiwis who, with the exception of John Reid, Bert Sutcliffe and captain Geoff Rabone, were weak and inexperienced. In the final Test at Port Elizabeth, throwing off the recently acquired 'Endless' tag, Endean demonstrated that when runs were required quickly, he was capable of producing fireworks. South Africa, chasing 212 in 225 minutes, lost three quick wickets before Endean and Watkins added 107 in 70 minutes, enabling the Springboks to romp to a five-wicket' victory with forty minutes to spare – Endean hitting 14 boundaries in his 87 made in ninety minutes.

Undoubtedly the most dramatic game of the one-sided series was the second Test starting on 24 December at Ellis Park, Johannesburg. On Boxing Day, New Zealand responding to the home side's 271 (Endean 93 – his highest score of the summer), were struggling against the fiery pace of the new Springbok fast bowler Neil Adcock, when news filtered through that Nerissa Love, fiancée of the Kiwi twenty-one-year-old fast bowler Bob Blair, was one of 151 people who had died in the Christmas Eve rail disaster at Tangiwai on New Zealand's North Island. The grieving Blair was holed up in the team hotel and not expected to take any further part in the game but, when the tourists' ninth wicket fell and the not out batsman, the heavily bandaged Sutcliffe (who had returned from hospital having earlier taken a severe blow behind the ear trying to hook an Adcock bouncer), started to leave the field, the forlorn and tearful figure of Blair unexpectedly appeared from the pavilion, to a deathly silence from the by now standing 23,000 crowd. Sutcliffe, after greeting Blair with a comforting arm round his shoulder, laid into Tayfield, hitting him for three sixes; this was followed, amid frenzied applause, by another six from

Bert Sutcliffe in the dramatic 2nd Test at Ellis Park

Blair. Twenty-five were scored from Tayfield's over, the most costly of his Test career. New Zealand eventually lost easily, but the match remains one of the most dramatic and poignant in the history of Test cricket. And, partly because of these tragic events, a particularly warm relationship developed between the two sides – New Zealand cricket writer Dick Brittenden recalled that 'they dined together, they went out together, they were the firmest of friends.' Russell Endean in later life was often seen wearing the black touring tie, with its silver fern motif, of his lifelong friend John Reid.

Because of the National Party's ever-tightening grip on South African politics, the only opponents the Springboks were allowed to play against were the all-white teams of New Zealand, England and Australia; they were denied fixtures against India, Pakistan and West Indies. But although it was in South Africa that pernicious racist divisions in sport were at their starkest, attitudes and norms were not so different in other parts of the world: Australia ruthlessly discriminated against her native Aborigine population and pursued a strict 'Whites only' immigration policy, while in the USA the major league baseball teams were almost exclusively all-white, with separate leagues for black teams. In his award-winning book about the Brooklyn Dodgers, *The Boys of Summer*, Roger Kahn describes the team's trip to Tampa: 'In 1952 apartheid flowered in the American hookworm belt. Blacks attended separate schools, patronized separate restaurants, drank at separate water fountains, relieved themselves at separate urinals, watching baseball from separate sections of the grandstand.' And, fuelled by the influx of West Indians to fill gaps in the labour market, prejudice in 1950s England was so rampant that the abused and discriminated-against immigrants took great joy in vocally supporting West Indian tourists; non-whites in South Africa similarly always cheered for the visiting teams.

Following the New Zealand tour, the summer of 1954/5 was devoted to a season of domestic cricket, before the selectors sat down to pick the Springboks' team to tour England. Endean had not been asked to continue leading Transvaal and under Ken Funston, the team finished runners-up to Natal in the A Section of the Currie Cup. In a prolific season, Endean's most stunning innings was at Ellis Park against Orange Free State (a team that included the hostile Peter Heine). He scored 235, 197 of which came before lunch; a possible double-century in the three-hour session being denied by his partner Cyril Tayfield (brother of Hugh) who played out the last over before the interval. Despite yo-yoing up and down the Transvaal batting-order, Endean came fifth in the first-class averages, scoring 541 runs at 60.11. A shoe-in for the 1955 tour of England, he next had to negotiate with his employers a five-month leave of absence.

****

The core of the team picked for the England campaign was made up of ten of the players who had done so well in the drawn series in Australia. Among the remaining six others, Neil Adcock and Peter Heine – two tall, lightning-quick opening bowlers – had taken 39 wickets between them in the six-match 1954/5 Currie Cup season. Adcock, in Transvaal's innings victory over Western Province on a lively Ellis Park pitch, had reduced the visitors to eight fit men, with opener Kevin Commins being carried unconscious from the field having been hit on the head by the fiery fast bowler. The tour committee was unchanged from Australasia, consisting of Ken Viljoen (manager), Jack Cheetham (captain), Jackie McGlew (vice-captain) and Russell Endean.

For a tour that was to have lasting significance in his life, it started for Endean in typically nonchalant fashion: he was still in bed when his best friend from school, Sandy Lawther, turned up to take him to Jan Smuts Airport where, for the first time, the team were travelling by air to England. Their new baggage master Mitchell McLennan (Bill Ferguson having retired after forty years serving touring teams), had sailed a week earlier with the team's trunks and cricket equipment. Flying in one of South African Airways' new Lockhead Constellations, the team left Johannesburg on 23 April. The leisurely flight, with detours to circle Kilimanjaro and Mont Blanc, required refuelling stops at Lusaka, Nairobi, Khartoum, Cairo, Athens, Rome and Paris, before some twenty-eight hours later it landed at London Airport under clear blue skies. Despite the news of recent apartheid atrocities filtering through to the British public – in March, 60,000 black South Africans were forcibly evicted from Sophiatown in order to make it a whites-only area – there was no sign of any protest when the Springboks arrived in England. Instead they were greeted by a group of distinguished, establishment figures, who included Lord Cobham, president of MCC; Ronnie Aird, secretary of MCC; and former England captain and member of the British Fascists, Arthur Gilligan. Tory peer Cobham had close connections with South Africa and within Prime Minister Anthony Eden's Conservative administration there were right-wing members who were strong supporters of the South African regime.

The team booked into the Park Lane Hotel, which as in 1951 was their well-appointed London base for the tour. With twelve days before the opening first-class game, this gave them plenty of time for nets at Lord's as well as a hectic round of socialising. With blue skies turning to grey soon after their arrival, the touring party often had to practice in soft and slippery conditions, with fast bowlers Heine and Adcock particularly hampered by the state of the run-ups. In between the rain the players, travelling by tube, visited sports outfitters Surridge and Slazenger to get kitted out and to choose their bats.

There is an evocative black-and-white press photograph of Russell Endean, in civvies, posing with a 'Perfect' bat in the front of Surridge's Borough High Street sports shop while, in the background, a group of passing, overalled workmen have their noses pressed up against the plate glass window.

Meanwhile new baggage-man McLennan was having his problems with British Customs – sixty pairs of cricket boots, not to mention a supply of South African cigarettes had been impounded. It took delicate negotiations as well as the coughing-up of some hefty duty charges before these essentials were released. The first Saturday of the tour was spent at the Empire Stadium, Wembley, watching the Rugby League Challenge Cup Final between Barrow and Workington Town. The first half was a dull affair, with the two Cumbrian teams swapping just one penalty apiece; but after the interval both sides produced some scintillating play with Barrow coming out winners by twenty-one points to twelve. Despite this sparkling second-half display, 'We were all rather disappointed at the manner in which the ball was kept by one side, who would rather lose twenty yards of ground than possession,' noted an unimpressed Jack Cheetham in his book about the tour, *I Declare.* 'I am quite confident that that Rugby League would not in any great way detract from the popularity of Rugby Union Football in South Africa.'

Russell Endean did not have happy memories of the 1951 tour. His form both as a batsman and as a keeper had been poor; and he had also found the constant travel from three-day match to three-day match, without any time to smell the roses, hard to cope with. The more measured itinerary around Australia had greater appeal to an intelligent man who liked to observe and study the land he found himself in. And no doubt it was this slower pace that allowed him to flourish as a cricketer on that tour. In 1955 he returned to England, a world-class performer at ease with his own talents and determined to improve on his earlier visit. But for Endean there was more to touring than cricket – as he had done on his first visit to England, he was quickly off the mark, pursuing his special interests in music and the theatre. In his first few days in the capital he crammed in visits to the Royal Festival Hall to hear the London Symphony Orchestra play a Beethoven programme, and to see Herbert von Karajan conduct the Philharmonia; he went to the Royal Opera House, Covent Garden for a performance of *The Bartered Bride*; to the St James's Theatre to see Margaret Leighton and Eric Portman star in Terence Rattigan's *Separate Tables*, the critically acclaimed double bill about sex and class; and to Sadler's Wells to watch Svetlana Beriosova and Beryl Grey in *Les Sylphides*. The broadcaster Charles Fortune recalled how shocked his team-mates were that Endean had gone to see a ballet.

Rain was beating on the carriage windows as the British Railways train took the South Africans to their first fixture at Worcester – where they

Endean in Stuart Surridge's Borough Road shop window

got off to the worst possible start, losing by 117 runs on a damp, spin-friendly pitch. The witheringly cold, three-sweater weather accompanied the tourists to their next rain-affected match against Derbyshire. In a game where they just managed to hold on for a draw, the press were starting to write off the tourists as no match for the unofficial world champions. 'They committed so many obvious elementary errors,' grumbled Denys Rowbotham in the *Manchester Guardian*, 'that it is impossible to judge them on normal first-class standards.' Although it was still so cold that a fire was kept blazing all day in the Trent Bridge dressing room, at least in the next drawn match against Nottinghamshire there was some batting form shown by both McGlew who made 88, and Endean, who played 'particularly brightly', for his 78. Overnight snow fell before the start of yet another drawn game at Fenner's against Cambridge University, but in the next game at Lord's, played out between icy showers of rain, a welcome 83-run victory was notched up against an England-strength MCC team. Fresh from his triumphant series in Australia, the home side were led by England captain Len Hutton who had recently become the first professional cricketer to be elected as an MCC honorary life member. A month short of his thirty-ninth birthday, the Yorkshireman played very little part in the game, retiring with an attack of lumbago brought on by the cold weather after making only two runs in the first innings, and not appearing at all in the second. Although appointed for all five of the forthcoming Tests against South Africa, illness kept him out of the entire series; and approaching middle-age and with nothing left to prove, he decided to end his distinguished England career.

The Springboks' victory went some way to silencing the non-stop criticism coming from the Fleet Street cricket writers; and their spirits were lifted further by rare warm weather for the game against Oxford University at Christ Church's Iffley Road ground – the tourists' game was always played away from The Parks so that a gate could be charged. In spring sunshine South Africa made a joyous 434-8, with a first century for the tourists from wicketkeeper John Waite, the Springboks going on to beat the Dark Blues by an innings. On the evening of 26 May – the second day of the match – while celebrating skipper Cheetham's thirty-fifth birthday in the team's hotel, they listened late into the night to the BBC Home Service programme *How the Country Polled*, with Andrew Shonfield and Alistair (*Letter from America*) Cooke analysing the early results of the General Election that eventually gave Anthony Eden's Conservative Party a comfortable 58-seat majority; and saw the cricket-loving Clement Attlee, whom a 2004 MORI poll would crown Britain's greatest prime minister of the twentieth century, retire as leader of the Labour Party.

After the first day of the next fixture against Glamorgan had been washed out, the South Africans in their only innings struggled on a damp pitch, off-spinner Jim McConnon tying them in knots while taking 6-49 in a twenty-five-over spell. Following the draw in Cardiff, the tourists, because of the recently called national rail strike, had to travel from the Welsh capital to Colchester by coach – a journey, through the winding roads of a Britain without motorways that took nine-and-a-half hours, the team arriving in their hotel at 3.30am. The next morning at the picturesque Castle Park ground, an unfamiliar warm sun greeted the captains – Essex's Doug Insole and Jackie McGlew. The acting Springboks' captain having called correctly – a good toss to win in every sense – took Endean out with him to open the South African innings. In perfect conditions the side batted for the whole first day and part of the second, before declaring on 504-4 (McGlew 118, McLean 101 not out, Mansell 99, Keith 94 and Endean 64). Essex were forced to follow on but the game ended in yet another draw. The last fixture before the first Test, against Lancashire, featured still more heavy rain, but between the downpours the Springboks' batsmen had some time in the middle: the tall, bespectacled right-hander Paul Winslow livened up the Saturday crowd, hitting 61 in the visitors' first innings, including 30 off one Jack Ikin over. And in the second innings Endean – being tried as an opener – Cheetham, Mansell and McLean all scored well before, with the score at 234-4, further heavy rain washed out the rest of the match. On the Saturday night some of the players had been to the variety show at Manchester's Palace Theatre starring the Pittsburgh-born jazz and pop singer Billy Eckstine; on the same bill the local comedian, attacking a popular target of the day, said to great applause: 'I'd like to bash my mother-in-law as Winslow bashed Ikin this afternoon.' Free tickets for such events were frequently laid on for the tourists, with each town and city they visited trying to make them welcome and show off their own particular virtues. So far they had attended official events at Worcester's City Hall; the Council Rooms at Derby; formal receptions at Lord's, South Africa House, and the British Sportsmen's Club lunch at the Savoy where, after taking some gentle chiding about the weakness of his team, Jack Cheetham replied that even that butt of music-hall jokes Chelsea had just become champions of the First Division, so there was hope for his team. There were visits to the television studios at Alexandra Palace where the players appeared in a BBC programme displaying their skills (Endean was chosen to demonstrate catching); and to Pinewood Studios to watch blonde bombshell Diana Dors (though some players said they preferred Marilyn Monroe's looks), and comedian and singer Norman Wisdom filming the Rank musical comedy *As Long as They're Happy*.

****

Norman Wisdom demonstrates his forward defensive outside the London Palladium

Cheetham leads out South Africa for the 1st Test at Trent Bridge

The Springboks arrived in Nottingham on 7 June two days before the start of the first Test. Preparations during the miserable early spring weather had left most of the team lacking form. Of the batsmen McGlew, despite a lingering hand injury, was easily the most consistent so far (503 runs at 62.87). The fast bowlers, particularly Heine, had struggled to find their rhythm on the damp run-ups, but Tayfield had revelled in the conditions and had taken 36 wickets at 16.25. Endean, who fitted in a visit to the Theatre Royal, Nottingham to see *The Remarkable Mr Pennypacker* starring Elizabeth Sellars and Nigel Patrick on the evening before the Test, was doing marginally better than four years earlier, with 318 runs at 28.9 in his eleven innings. His father William had made the trip from South Africa, and along with Jack Cheetham's mother and Paul Winslow's father, was present at Trent Bridge for the start of the Test. Peter May, captaining in place of the unwell Hutton, won the toss; and his batsmen, although never dominating the steady South African attack, did not let him down, finishing the day on 244-4. Only the twenty-four-year-old Surrey debutant Ken Barrington failed, unlucky enough to get one of the few balls all day that lifted, and was out for a duck, caught by Waite standing up to the fast-medium Eddie Fuller off the fourth ball he faced. He joined a distinguished group, Len Hutton and Graham Gooch amongst them, who have made nought in their first Test innings – this trio would go on to become three of England's greatest post-war batsmen.

Waiting for the second day's play to get under way, the South Africans huddled round the dressing-room fire plotting how to dismiss May and England's middle and lower order. In fact May added only another two runs but, thanks to the obdurate Trevor Bailey and some long-handle strokes by the tail, the home side reached 334 (Kenyon 89, May 83) soon after lunch. The light was poor – Alan Ross described it as 'tunnel-like darkness' in the *Observer* – and with no sightscreens at either end of the ground, conditions were tough for Jackie McGlew and Trevor Goddard when they went out to face Brian Statham and Frank Tyson. The Northants' typhoon was bowling particularly fast – 'I'd never seen anyone so quick in all my life,' was Goddard's verdict in Trevor Quirk's film *Springboks Cricket Saga*. But it was Statham who broke the opening partnership, trapping Goddard lbw for 12. There then followed a disastrous run out – John Waite, turning for a third run, was a yard short as a Statham bullet throw winged into Evans's gloves. As Russell Endean walked slowly to the crease, eyeing the lowering clouds, he must have wished he could have appealed against the light. But, at the request of the MCC (controllers of cricket in England), the South African Cricket Association had agreed that the umpires should be the sole arbiters of playing conditions. Endean, not happy with movement behind the bowler's arm, had twice drawn away; but padding up to his third ball from Tyson, he was comprehensively beaten by a fast break-back and was lbw for nought, leaving South Africa 19-3. Dour batting from the Springboks' captain Cheetham and vice-captain McGlew saw their side through to close at 83-5.

On the following day the 15,000 Saturday crowd watched patiently under cool and cloudy conditions while the overnight batsmen, somewhat battered by the previous evening's hostile bowling, took the South African total to within 35 runs of avoiding the follow-on before the sixth wicket fell, but the remaining tail-enders' contribution fell four runs short – South Africa making 181 (McGlew 68, Cheetham 54). Despite the bruising pace of England's fast men, it was the parsimonious spin bowling of Yorkshiremen Johnny Wardle (4-24) and Bob Appleyard (2-46) that had taken the majority of the wickets. Following on, South Africa were blown away by Tyson, who in 21.3 overs took 6-24. Only McGlew (53) and Goddard (32) in an opening partnership of 73 put up any resistance. South Africa were all out for 148 and had lost by an inning and five runs. A *Central Press* black-and-white photograph of Endean's dismissal – caught in the slips off Bailey for just six – shows the inhospitable conditions: the grassed pitch is hardly distinguishable from the rest of the square, the crease is scarred with dark footholds and is covered in mounds of sawdust, while the players are huddled in long-sleeved sweaters to protect them from the cold winds.

1st Test: Endean ct Graveney b Bailey 6

After the match Endean was one of the brains trust who, analysing the overwhelming defeat, came to the conclusion that there was a need for the Springboks to answer fire with fire. That meant picking both their fast bowlers, Heine (who had been left out in preference to medium-pacer Fuller) and Adcock for the second Test, and making greater use of the short-pitched ball and the bouncer.

****

The following day's coach journey from Trent Bridge to Taunton for the next county fixture took eight hours. But the day after their arrival, news came through that the rail strike had been cancelled and the subsequent journey from Taunton to Hove was made on a luxurious British Railways train. Played in welcoming warm sunshine, the tourist chalked up victories against Somerset and Sussex, with several batsmen – making the most of the firm pitches – scoring heavily: Cheetham made 87 not out in the West Country; and McLean 129, Endean 73 not out, McGlew 69 and Waite 53 on the South Coast. Jim Parks and David Sheppard (not yet frocked) made centuries for Sussex in a losing cause. The day before the start of the second Test, the tourists practised in the morning before taking the District Line to Wimbledon where they were to be guests of the All England Club for the third day of the Championships. They had lunch with chairman Mr AH Risely and met the Duchess of Kent in the Royal Box – captain Cheetham and manager Viljoen were each granted fifteen minutes sitting next to Her Royal Highness – and saw holder Jaroslav Drobny and Lew Hoad win their second round Men's Singles matches (the crew-cut American Tony Trabert would beat the Dane Kurt Nielsen in the final the following week). The tournament's two-shillings-and-sixpence programme featured on its front cover Coventry-born England number one Tony Mottram, who two weeks before had enjoyed the ultimate accolade of being interviewed by Roy Plomley on *Desert Island Discs*. Among his eight choices he included the Polish Army Choir singing *The Road to the Isles* and Fats Waller playing *Alligator Crawl*.

The decision to select both Adcock and Heine for the Lord's Test (which was, like Wimbledon, one of the events of 'The Season') proved wise. MCC Secretary Ronnie Aird had promised a fast pitch, and the strip was as 'green as a Hampshire water meadow,' wrote John Woodcock in *The Times*, 'so green in fact that one could hardly identify it from the outfield, and it was well grassed into the bargain.' On top of which it was a muggy and grey day, which made May's decision to bat a strange one. In just over three hours South Africa skittled England out for 133. Debutant Peter Heine's first wicket was that of May himself, caught at third slip by Tayfield for nought from a ball that reared off a length and caught the shoulder – a typical delivery in a hostile spell that saw the six-foot-four Orange Free State fast bowler finish with figures of 5-60. Ken Barrington top-scored for England, grinding out 34 in an hour-and-a-half stay at the crease. In the remains of the day, South Africa got off to a calamitous start: McGlew was out first ball of the innings, caught Evans bowled Statham; and Goddard was also out for nought, again caught by the keeper, this time off Fred Trueman, in for the injured Tyson. But the Springboks fought back. Coming in at number four with the score at 7 for 2, Endean played some powerful cuts and drives before, to the surprise of the away dressing-room, three yards down the wicket to Wardle, he was given out lbw for a defiantly played 48. But the innings that sent the 25,000 crowd home purring was McLean's undefeated 62, made in the last hour of the day's play, with his side finishing 142-5 at stumps. In front of a full house – many of them sitting on the grass – McLean carried on in the same vein on day two, hammering 142 in his side's impressive total of 304. But England, with undefeated half-centuries from Tom Graveney and May, went serenely to 108-1 at the close of play.

The next day, thanks to a masterful 112 by May and a vintage 69 from Compton that included, according to John Woodcock, 'some of the best batting that has come from an English pair in adversity since the War', England reached a more than respectable 353, setting South Africa 183 for victory. By the end of the day the visitors had been reduced to 17-2 (McGlew avoiding a king pair by one ball) and the departing crowd, that included two of England's greatest bowlers, SF Barnes and Wilfred Rhodes, must have felt that with the fall of those late wickets the odds had tipped in the home side's favour. Not out at the close, and aware that Cheetham was unlikely to bat after having taken a sickening blow to the elbow, Endean chose to relax on Sunday (as usual, a rest day) and in the evening crossed the Thames for an evening concert at the Festival Hall given by the Philharmonia Orchestra. As well as Beethoven's 8th and two nocturnes by Debussy, the programme finished with Respighi's tone poem *The Pines of Rome*, a poignant reminder of where Russell had celebrated the end of the war.

It turned out to be a torrid Monday for South Africa: heavy clouds all day, two hours lost to bad light and drizzle, and Statham at his metronomic 'If you miss, I hit' best. The visitors never looked like scoring the remaining 166 needed to level the series. Endean was top scorer with a gritty 28, but once the first-innings hero McLean had played rashly across the line to a good-length delivery from Statham, the rest of the Springboks offered only token resistance – all out for 111, they lost by 71 runs. In retirement Endean recalled that it was 'a hard grassy wicket – did the so-called ridge ever really exist? – and it was Statham (29-12-39-7) with his great accuracy and control who had won the match for England.' It had been an absorbing and fluctuating Test that over the four days had been watched by 103,000 people; but having had such a commanding lead on first innings, the visitors must have felt they had missed out. Two-down in the series with three to play, their tour was in danger of unravelling. Jack Cheetham would subsequently raise the question of poor (or biased) umpiring: as well as Endean's lbw in the first innings, he wrote of the refusal of Trevor Bailey to walk after he had edged the ball to slip, where it had been cleanly caught by Percy Mansell. The Essex all-rounder had stood his ground; and after umpires Laurie Gray and Frank Chester had consulted, the aptly named 'Barnacle' was given not out. Cheetham quotes Mansell: 'It was a fair catch. Do I look like a cheat?'

The early finish to the Test gave the tourists an extra day in London to sample what the capital had to offer. Some of the players went to watch some tennis at the second week of Wimbledon, while others went with Jack Cheetham and his mother to the Victoria Palace to see the Crazy Gang (Bud Flanagan; Nervo & Knox; Naughton & Gold) plus the high-kicking John Tiller Girls in the musical revue *Jokers Wild*. The highbrow Russell Endean took the opportunity to see *Moby Dick* at the Duke of York's Theatre. Orson Welles, who wrote and directed the production, played Captain Ahab, and the remainder of the cast included some of Britain's leading actors: Christopher Lee, Kenneth Williams, Joan Plowright (as Pip, the mad cabin boy), Patrick McGoohan, Gordon Jackson, Peter Sallis and Wensley Pithey. 'If British audiences wish to exert themselves, to have their minds set whirling and their eyes dazzling at sheer theatrical virtuosity,' wrote the *Observer*'s Kenneth Tynan, '*Moby Dick* is their opportunity. With it, the theatre becomes once more a house of magic.' Endean did well to catch this play, as it only ran for three weeks; Welles intended it eventually to be filmed for US television, but in the event, after just one day of shooting at Hackney Empire (where the author spent his first day as a TV cameraman in 1960), the project was abandoned, with what was filmed unfortunately lost. Happy to spend more time in London, Endean did not play in the comfortable victory against Northamptonshire but was a member of the team that achieved their best result of the tour so far – beating a strong Yorkshire team (only Hutton was absent) at a gloomy Bramall Lane, Sheffield by a resounding 193 runs. Hugh Tayfield was the outstanding performer, taking eight wickets in the match and top-scoring with 65 in the South African second innings (Endean, still struggling with the bat, managed only 2 and 16).

The Third Test, started on 7 July at Old Trafford, and was played in a heatwave, more like Durban than Manchester. Cheetham was unfit so it was Jackie McGlew who went out to toss with Peter May. The wicket was 'a beauty' according to the groundsman, and the Surrey amateur, having won the toss, had no hesitation in electing to bat first. England had lost four wickets for 89 at lunch, with Compton and Bailey the not out batsmen. One

An injured Cheetham wishes stand-in captain McGlew good luck for 3rd Test

of the England top-order back in the pavilion, dismissed for a single, was Colin Cowdrey, the young Kent amateur who earlier in the summer had been allowed to cut short his National Service because of a history of 'foot trouble'. Appearing on a cricket field looking so fit and healthy only weeks after being discharged from the RAF, he received a sackful of hate mail, as well as an attack from handlebar-moustached Conservative MP Gerald Nabarro who accused him in the Commons of 'dodging the column'. To try and redress the balance Cowdrey, wearing a Kent blazer and sweater, appeared on a British Pathé newsreel taking off his sock to show his right foot with the stiffened big toe ('it might be a bit smelly') and saying: 'A month ago I signed on. I'm now discharged and here I am rather helpless. What do you want me to do – volunteer again?' England finished day-one on 264-7, the South African bowlers doing well to restrict the home side to just over two runs an over, but the Springboks could not contain a dominant Denis Compton who was 155 not out at the close. The Brylcreem Boy's wonderful innings had delighted the sun-drenched crowd of shirt-sleeved men, and summer frocked women, who marvelled at his dancing footwork as he chasséd up and down the wicket to Tayfield, trying to unsettle the unremitting off spinner – it was vintage Compton.

A tight second day was edged by South Africa. The remaining three England wickets fell quickly: Compton was the first to go for 158 and the side finishing on a below-par 284, with Heine, Adcock and Goddard each taking three wickets apiece. The rest of the day, another scorcher, was attritional. Built round Goddard and McGlew's opening stand of 147, South Africa were 199-4 at the close of play. On Saturday, with the dismissal of Headley Keith for 38, and their score at 245-5, the Springboks looked as though their advantage was slipping away. But all was to change in the next three hours. The huge Mancunian crowd was treated to one of the most memorable Test match innings ever seen at Old Trafford. Next in to join John Waite, batting at number eight, was the six-foot-four Paul Winslow, son of national tennis champions Olive and Charles (a double Olympic gold medallist at Oslo in 1912). The crowd greeted him warmly, remembering his hitting in the county match. He played himself in cautiously until, just before lunch, he straight drove Bailey for the first six of the match. There was no more circumspection after lunch – in the first over, Winslow cut and cover-drove Tony Lock for two boundaries. All the England bowlers were put to the sword with the most thrilling of all the shots being a pull for six off a Tyson thunderbolt that, with the members cowering, rattled into the pavilion pickets. Winslow was 92 not out when Lock started the last over before tea; he square cut him for four before striding down the pitch to the fifth ball and striking the Surrey left-arm spinner for a memorable straight six that landed in the car park fifty yards beyond the boundary. As he returned to the pavilion, the whole ground stood to greet the twenty-six-year-old who had chosen a Test match to notch his first first-class century. He was out soon after the break for 108, but the runs continued to flow – Waite making 113 and McGlew (who had had to retire hurt on 70 on the third day) taking his score to 104 before declaring his side's innings closed at 521 for 8. England batted solidly in their second innings, a classy May century backed up by 71 from Compton and exactly 50 from a sure-footed Cowdrey. Nevertheless they were dismissed late in the afternoon session on day five for 381 (Heine 5-86), leaving South Africa to score 145 in 135 minutes. Thanks to a tardy over rate and a leisurely drinks break, England had managed only 30.3 overs when Waite hit the winning boundary with just four minutes to spare – McGlew having made a steady 48, McLean a quick fire 50, and Winslow 16 (two sixes and a four) in eight balls. Alec Bedser, in what proved to be the swansong in a truly great Test career, was hammered in the run chase, taking 2-61 in his ten overs (4-154 in the match). 'It had been a spectator's Test match,' recalled John Waite, 'five wonderful days.' But for Russell Endean it had been an undistinguished match: as well as uncharacteristically dropping a straightforward catch, he was dismissed twice by Lock for 5 and 2.

The match will always be remembered for Paul Winslow's breath-taking century, but for the young man from Johannesburg even more significant was a tryst that had taken place in the East Midlands earlier in the tour. Eleven actresses invited eleven Springboks to the Derby Playhouse to see their play *Women of Twilight*. At the drinks party after the show Winslow fell for one of the cast, the twenty-three-year-old elfin beauty Moira Gray. Ten days later they were engaged, and on 22 October they married at the Congregational Church in Purley before travelling back to South Africa together. After the romantic start to their married life, and the birth of four children, their lives would be shattered by two devastating tragedies. In 1977 their eighteen-year-old daughter, Carey, died of lupus; eight years later, their twenty-eight-year-old daughter Lucy, thirteen-year-old son Peter and two grandchildren, Richard and Craig, were all killed in a road accident. *No Time for Goodbyes*, a moving documentary made in 2010, tells the story. In the film Paul Winslow says: 'I don't think a day goes by that I don't recall some form of it.' And so overcome was he by the memories of his loss that he became something of a recluse. Moira Winslow on the other hand, after her heartbreaking experience, said: 'I'm tough. I coped. What else can you do?' And this resilience drove her on to become a pioneering road safety activist – she started Drive Alive, a highly successful awareness campaign that is still working with children into the twenty-first century, particularly in the poorer parts of South Africa where children continue to walk along main roads to school.

✳✳✳✳✳✳✳✳✳✳✳✳

The victorious South Africans left Manchester on the midnight sleeper train, arriving in London on the morning that Albert Pierrepoint carried out the execution by hanging of Ruth Ellis at Holloway Prison. The twenty-eight-year-old working-class woman, one-time prostitute and nightclub hostess, had been convicted of shooting her abusive lover, the public schoolboy, racing driver David Blakely who, a week before the murder, had caused Ruth to miscarry by punching her in the stomach. Ellis's execution – the last woman to suffer such a fate in Britain – divided the nation. 'This was a crime of passion under considerable provocation,' wrote Raymond Chandler in a letter to the *Evening Standard*, 'No other country in the world would hang this woman.'

The South African captain's only slowly recovering elbow injury, and the vice-captain's swollen right hand, meant that Endean was called on to captain the Springboks against Surrey at the Oval. Happy to be back in London, he had managed a trip to Her Majesty's Theatre to see the Pulitzer Prize winning drama *The Teahouse of the August Moon*. The heatwave was still enveloping Britain and, fresh from their two impressive victories, the

South Africans relished taking on the county champions. The first day was dominated by a dazzling innings of 151 from Roy McLean, who completely tamed the all-conquering attack of twins Alec and Eric Bedser, Jim Laker and Peter Loader. Despite innings of 62 and 43 from Peter May, Surrey were bowled out twice on a typical wearing Bert Lock wicket for under 200, and lost by 82 runs, Tayfield finishing with match figures of 13-98. The tourists' stand-in captain, although he only contributed scores of 30 and 0 in the match, must have taken a great deal of satisfaction in beating the team who would that season go on to win the County Championship for the fourth time in succession. On the second day of the match the players met the Queen at the Oval. The visit was covered by Pathé, whose black-and-white newsreel, as well as showing the Queen meeting the cricketers, filmed her dutifully exchanging a few words with a group of Kennington pensioners living in what was then a very deprived part of South London. Like every overseas cricketer, Russell Endean's archive includes a photograph of himself, second in line, bowing respectfully as he shakes the gloved hand of the young monarch. The whole touring party (lined-up in descending height order) were immaculately turned out in their green-and-gold blazers, and Jack Cheetham had discarded his sling to introduce his players. Overawed in her presence, he later wrote in hallowed terms of that 'charm and indefinable quality which one instinctively feels when in the presence of royalty.'

****

Buoyed by their run of three successive victories, the tourists travelled north in the hope of making it four in a row and levelling the series. The Leeds Test started on 21 July in front of a Thursday crowd of 21,000, attracted by continuing hot weather and the resurgence of the visitors' form. South Africa stuck with the winning eleven from Old Trafford, so it was Jackie McGlew who won the toss and chose to bat on what looked like a plumb surface. His side made poor use of the pristine pitch, though, and were dismissed before the close for an underwhelming 171. At one time they were 63 for 6, and only two scores of 41 – one from the in-form McLean, the other from the decidedly out-of-form Endean, batting at a lowly number eight in the order – got the total to semi-respectability. This Springboks' collapse was mitigated to some extent by the dismissal of England's openers Lowson and Bailey, leaving England 25-2 at the close.

On day two, thanks to consistently outstanding run-saving fielding and fine bowling from Heine and Tayfield who both finished with figures of 4-70, England were dismissed for a barely more respectable 191 (Compton 61, May 47), six of their order falling lbw. When stumps were drawn at the end of the day, McGlew and Goddard had consolidated South Africa's position in the game with an unbroken opening stand of 107. 26,000 Yorkshire men and women were ready for the start of play on day three. 'The sun was again high over a crowd whose blobs of colour were as closely packed as in a Frith painting,' wrote Alan Ross in the *Observer*. 'A few sierras of stationary cloud lay above the grimy red roofs and screen of intervening poplars planted a quarter century ago to prevent free observation from the Kirkstall Lane end.' There was ample time for reveries, as on a mundane and uneventful day the visitors – not to the liking of the restless Yorkshire throng – very sedately advanced their score to 341-5 (McGlew 133, Goddard 74, Keith 73).

Monday, in front of a remarkable 36,000 Headingley crowd, turned out to be a long-awaited glory day for Russell Endean who finished 116 not out when South Africa's second innings closed at exactly 500. He had scored 99 of the 159 added on day four; mainly batting with the tail, and on a pitch that was taking sharp spin, he played 'the dour, commonsense, efficient innings one had been fearing all the season Endean would play,' noted an admiring Denys Rowbotham in the *Manchester Guardian* 'A Yorkshire crowd was the right crowd to appraise it.' They would have admired this steely four-hour innings that perhaps owed something to his mother's white-rose genes. Although based on defence, there were sixteen boundaries – he was always quick to cut Bailey and Statham the moment they pitched slightly short; he

*4th Test: Endean cuts Statham past Compton for four
during innings of 116 not out*

incisively hooked a Wardle long-hop to reach his hundred, and then twice 'hammer-drove' Bailey square for fours.

England had two hours batting left on day four and the whole of the last day to score the 481 needed for victory – 'the greatest feat in Test history if England pull it off,' was Crawford White's hyperbolic verdict in the *News Chronicle*. The home side finished the day on 115-2, the not-out batsmen being the two Cambridge blues, May with 47 and Doug Insole on 30. The pugnacious Essex amateur, in his only game of the series, adopted an effective method of playing Tayfield that he was to put to great effect eighteen months later in South Africa. Despite having only three fit bowlers – Adcock, with a broken bone in his foot, was unable to field, and Heine was limping – South Africa never let England get close to their target, dismissing them for 256 (May 97) with over two hours left in the day. Two bowlers with remarkable match-winning spells – Goddard, 62-37-69-5, and Tayfield, 47.1-15-94-5 – had ensured a comprehensive 224-run victory for the Springboks. 'At the corner of the main street in Johannesburg, traffic was held up for a time by a crowd of about 500 who spread across the pavement and into the roadway while listening to a commentary outside a radio shop,' reported Reuters. 'As England's last wicket fell the cheers of the listeners echoed around the streets' Showing the indomitable team spirit that had been developed in Australia two years earlier, the tourists had become the first South African team to win two Tests in England. The series was all-square, with everything to play for at the Oval.

****

The defeated England eleven was an amalgam of Gentleman and Players, as it had been since the nineteenth century, and an article in *The Times* on the last day of the fourth Test was a reminder that class divisions were still significant in 1950s Britain. 'The Paper of Record' reported that Denis Howell MP (he would later to be Minister of Sport in Harold Wilson's Labour Government) had raised in the House of Commons that batmen at RAF Halton, Buckinghamshire are being used as domestic helps for the officers' wives – they have to clean windows, cut lawns, polish floors, run errands, and fetch in coal; in one or two cases batmen have been expected to dress officers' children and take them to school.

****

To the relief of manager Ken Viljoen, and thanks to the overflowing 36,000 fourth-day crowd at Headingley, the tour had now broken even; but, in order to run up a surplus, the South Africans had to continue to criss-cross the country – playing five more fixtures in the less than three weeks before the deciding Test at the Oval. The rampant Springboks, still basking in the continuing heatwave, had overwhelming victories against

Glamorgan, Warwickshire and Leicestershire as well as drawn games against Gloucestershire and a Minor Counties XI. Endean, wearying of the non-stop travel, asked for and was given a rest from cricket. He came back refreshed from a short walking holiday in the Lake District and hit somewhere near his best form – he scored 250 runs in his next five knocks including an aggressive 98 on a dusty Edgbaston wicket against a Warwickshire team that included Don Bradman's nemesis, Eric Hollies. On the Sunday of the Bank Holiday fixture at Swansea, Jack Cheetham drove to Badminton to play in a match to raise money for the National Playing Fields Association; and to meet royalty again. Along with Jackie McGlew, he had been invited to play for the Duke of Edinburgh ('a charming personality and a born leader') against the Duke of Beaufort's XI. Prince Philip, who – ahead of his time – wore sunglasses to bat and field, scored a spoon-fed 22 in his side's four-wicket victory.

The South Africans, while travelling down from Leicester on Friday evening, only some twenty hours before the start of the Test, contemplated what was the best eleven to play in the decisive match. It was felt that Neil Adcock's damaged foot could not be risked and Paul Winslow had lost form after his stunning Old Trafford innings – perhaps spending too much time pining for

Nibbles at Rhodesia House before the Final Test
left to right: Endean, Eddie Fuller, and Middlesex's Alan Moss & Fred Titmus

his Scottish actress. The trickiest decision was whether Jack Cheetham should resume as captain. The senior players persuaded him to play, news which did not go down well with everybody back home – his wife receiving many anonymous phone calls questioning her husband's right to be in the side. Such behaviour was an indication of the enormous South African interest in the match; Cheetham received a telegram in Afrikaans from Mr Ben Scheoman, the Minister of Railways, which in translation read 'Last month I laid a big African elephant low in Bechuanaland. All railway men join with me in hoping that you and your team will at least fell eleven little Lions at the Oval. Good Luck.' England's hands-on selectors also made changes – with only four players surviving from Leeds, a response the newspapers described as 'panicky'.

People had been queuing all-night to watch the Test, and when the Springboks arrived at the Oval there were still huge crowds circling the outside of the brick-walled ground. May won his fourth toss of the series and decided to bat on a pitch that, although notorious for taking spin later in a match, had an unfamiliar green tinge at the start of the game. Now mostly wearing long-sleeved sweaters – the heat wave having given way to cooler weather and grey skies – the South Africans came with a clatter down the stone steps of the Victorian pavilion, through the white boundary gate, and onto the largest

5th Test, South Africa take the field: (left to right) Keith, McLean, Goddard, Waite, Tayfield, Mansell, Cheetham, Heine, McGlew, Endean, Fuller

playing area in England. Unfortunately for the expectant 30,000 crammed into the Kennington ground, the day was an anti-climax – less than three hours of play was possible after a cloudburst flooded the uncovered wicket, with England on 70 for 3. The two most notable events of the truncated day were the cheap dismissal of skipper May – neatly caught for 3 at second slip by Goddard off the bowling of the medium-pacer Fuller – and the veteran Lancashire opener Jack Ikin being painfully hit in the stomach by a rising ball from Neil Adcock, a blow that re-opened a recently stitched surgical wound. Ikin was one of a cluster of left-handed batsmen (Close, Watson and keeper Spooner the others) whom the England selectors had brought in to counter Goddard's leg-stump line of attack. After more rain on Sunday, the wicket on Monday morning was far livelier, and England were bundled out soon after lunch for 151 (Close 32, Compton 30, Goddard 5-31, Tayfield 3-39). The South Africans, after two months of batting on hard strips, were no match for Lock and Laker who, bowling on a pitch that seemed made for them, shot out the Springboks for 112 (McGlew 30). A *Central Press* black-and-white photograph shows Russell Endean's dismissal for a duck: a 'vicious' ball from Lock has 'turned and kicked', the batman has been squared-up, and he is looking over his right shoulder to gully where Ikin at has bagged the catch, while at the other end Lock in typically histrionic fashion, has raised his head and arms to the sky.

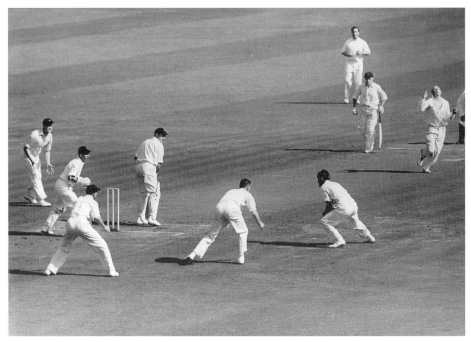

5th Test: Endean caught Ikin bowled Lock 0

England, starting their second inning first thing on Tuesday morning, then batted all day, finishing with a hard-fought score of 194-8. A match-turning incident happened with the score at 39-2; Hugh Tayfield, who was at the start of what would be a marathon five-hour spell, flighted a full-length ball to Peter May, who played back and was hit below the knee. Waite and the bowler confidently appealed for what they thought was a certain lbw, but were stunned when umpire Tom Bartley looked away. The volatile Tayfield's next ball was a fast and angry high full-toss, which May crashed to the boundary. The young Surrey amateur went on to score 89 not out and England were dismissed early on day four for 204, setting South Africa an unlikely 244 for victory. They were never able to put together any substantial partnerships and were dismissed for 151 (Waite 60, Lock 5-62, Laker 4-56), England winning by 92 runs. In this final innings of the series

there were three more controversial umpiring decisions that were to cause much resentment amongst the Springboks for many years to come. The trilby-hatted Bartley gave Keith, McLean and Endean (bagging a pair) all out lbw while sweeping at Laker. A press photograph of McLean's dismissal (also out for nought), while not conclusive, shows his front leg well outside off-stump. Jackie McGlew, the non-striker during these dismissals, reckoned subsequently that 'we had got a raw deal – they were roughies.' Speaking in Trevor Quirk's 1992 film, he was convinced that 'on a turning wicket, turning almost at right angles, and on the sweep, it just wasn't on. I'm convinced about that. Today the guys would not be given out.' 'It was most unfortunate that potentially such a fine game was clouded by controversy,' wrote Brian Bassano in

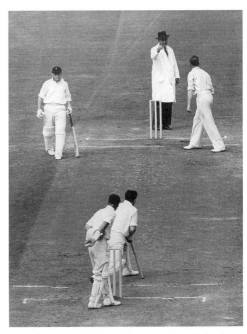

5th Test: McLean the second of Laker's three second innings lbw victims. A sceptical McGlew looks on

1996, articulating the resentment that had festered for over forty years. 'Few will deny that the Springboks were the victims of at least three extremely bad decisions, one of which probably cost them the match.' And even Russell Endean, always very reluctant to criticise umpires, many years later said that he thought decisions during the final Test had cost South Africa the match and the series.

Endean's melancholy at his side's defeat and his failure to score a single run in the final Test was soon to be lifted. Two faces in the final day crowd belonged to a couple of confident young women – more interested in the eligible Peter May's good looks than Jim Laker's arm-ball or Denis Compton's flick off his legs – had wangled their way into a party to celebrate the end of the series. For one of the friends, Muriel Tredwell, her head was turned not by the England captain but by the handsome profile of Russell Endean, and he was equally infatuated.

The striking twenty-seven-year-old Muriel certainly lifted Endean's spirits during the last month of the tour. In the final first-class match at Scarborough against T.N. Pearce's XI, he scored 138 not out in three hours against a bowling attack of Trueman, Bedser, Bailey, Close and Wardle, his best innings of the tour. The smitten batsman also made 46 against Hampshire at Southampton, and 75 and 39 against Middlesex at Lord's. He ended with 1,242 runs at an average of 34.5 on the tour; but apart from his century at Leeds, his contributions in the Tests were disappointing, scoring 246 at 27.33. Despite the setback in the last Test, the Springboks finished the summer with a string of convincing victories. On the tour they won 15 of their 28 first-class matches; nine were left drawn, and only four were lost. The team's outstanding performers were the intrepid and consistent Jackie McGlew, who topped the national averages, scoring 1,871 at 58.47; and the phenomenal Tayfield with 143 wickets at 15.74. The tourists had been well-led by their ever-gracious captain, Jack Cheetham, and the manager Ken Viljoen, their behind-the-scenes masseur, psychologist and accountant. Altogether, the tour made a profit of some £36,000. This allowed the South African Board to pay the players an additional £150 allowance to cover the high cost of living while they were in England. To cap it all, the highly popular South African team were presented with a cup by film star Anna Neagle at a gala dinner at The Savoy, for their outstanding performances during the summer. Through their infectious enthusiasm, fighting spirit and breath-taking fielding, the South Africans left England having made many new friends; and for two of the team they had found more than friendship.

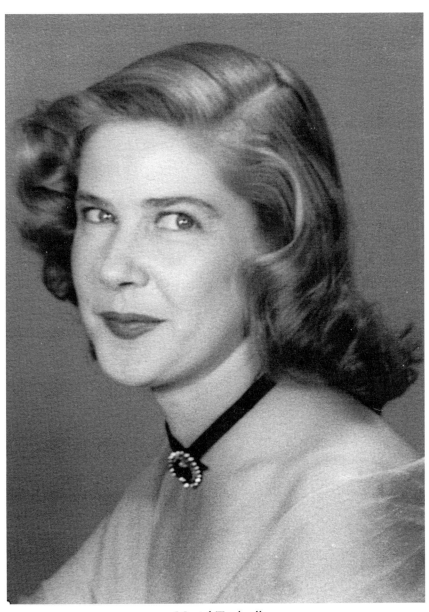

Muriel Tredwell

Chapter Five

Muriel's Wedding

For Russell Endean and Muriel Tredwell their attraction was more than a passing fancy. So certain of a future together were they that, before Russell flew back to South Africa, he was taken to Edith Road, Fulham to meet Muriel's mother Maud. But what of the woman whom Russell left behind? Muriel Daphne Tredwell was born on 14 October 1927 (over three years younger than her new beau) at 34 Burnfoot Avenue, a stone's throw from Craven Cottage, the home of Fulham Football Club. On her birth certificate her father Mark described himself as a lorry driver; and she had three older siblings: Violet, Cecil and James.

Muriel had an exceptionally colourful collection of ancestors. Their riches-to-rags story included her great grandfather Solomon Tredwell, a Victorian engineering-contractor who worked with Isambard Kingdom Brunel on the building of the revolutionary paddle steamer *The Great Eastern*. In 1859 he went out to India to work on the construction of the Bombay-to-Poona section of the Great Indian Peninsula Railway. But two months into the assignment he died of dysentery aged thirty-four. Solomon's wife, Alice (who inherited £70,000 on the death of her husband), was a woman ahead of her time: having travelled to the sub-continent with Solomon, she took over the project, employing new engineers and overseeing the completion of the railway in 1863.

There were two children from this marriage: a daughter Alice, and a son Mark John, Muriel's grandfather. Aged ten, his mother died and Mark inherited the family's considerable fortune. A sickly child, now living with his maternal grandmother, Mark went first to Cheam School (which is nowhere near Cheam and where Prince Charles was a pupil) before going to Harrow. He was only seventeen when he met Polly Wentworth; she – 'several years his senior' – seduced him, and

Alice Tredwell
the accidental railway engineer

then married him at St Gabriel's Church, Pimlico (the marriage certificate gave his age as twenty-one). It was only when his friends recognised the bride as Polly Ward alias Polly Campbell, who was married to the comedian Frederick Wentworth Gray, that at the Divorce Division of the High Court, in front of Judge Sir James Hannen, the jury found in favour of the adolescent and the Court pronounced a decree nisi for nullity of the brief marriage. Mark's wealth remained intact after this narrow squeak, but he was still in delicate health so chose to start a new life in the fresh-air of mid-Wales. In this rural outpost, the metropolitan young man proceeded to spend his money lavishly: he bought and renovated Aberllolwyn, a mansion on the shores of Llyn Eiddwen, an upland lake three miles south of Aberystwyth; and on a small island on the lake, he built a hugely costly castle. In Mark's four years in Wales he spent so recklessly on his various follies that when he left the principality, he had blown the majority of his fortune. One other outcome of this Welsh interlude was an affair with Caroline Smith. Together they had several children, one of whom a boy, born in 1881, was named Mark Tredwell. This was Muriel's father. While the young Mark was being brought up by his maternal grandparents in Brighton, his father, Muriel's grandfather, was carrying on in his merry way. His next conquest was the Peruvian Consol General's daughter, Mercedes de la Quintana with whom he had two children: yet another Mark, and a daughter Beatrice. In Muriel's grandfather's long, freewheeling life, he had relationships and children with five different women but, perhaps not surprisingly, by the time of his death in 1930 nothing remained of the hard-won Tredwell family fortune.

When Muriel came into the world, her parents were living very much in the lower echelons of London society. Their house in working-class Fulham (now gentrified) suffered bomb damage during the Second World War, and the family were billeted in a Victorian house owned by the Warsaw-born artist Josef Herman – a distinguished social-realist painter, famous for his pictures of working-class life, particularly Welsh coalminers. The Tredwells lived in cramped conditions on the second floor, sharing a bathroom and lavatory with a Miss Prior who was on the ground floor; Herman chose to live at the top of the house where the light was at its best. Despite losing her father – he died aged 56 when she was ten – Muriel prospered in a loving family. First educated at Heathfield House School, Fulham, she passed the entrance exam to Tiffin Girls, a grammar school in Kingston upon Thames. Tiffin – still in the twenty-first century using the 11+ exam to separate the sheep from the goats – is now one of the most prestigious state schools in Britain. For a grammar school girl like Muriel who did not make it to university, and precious few did, office work was a safe but limiting option after the war. On leaving school she trained as a secretary,

Muriel, the girl about town

and with her newly acquired shorthand and typing skills had no trouble in finding well-paid work in London. At the beginning of 1955, aged 27 and still living at home, she was working at 168 Regent Street for agents H.S.A & Campbell Ltd, a Black Country firm that distributed the Dudley-built bicycle, the 'Mercury Roadster', to the USA. A carefree girl-about-town with leftish leanings (possibly influenced by artist Josef Herman), she was a frequent party and cinema goer, wore fashionable Dior-style clothes and had many good friends, although a 'Mr Right' was still to come along. A sympathetic letter from 'Slady', a friend living in Surbiton, highlights the problem: 'Sorry to hear about you and Don. What happened? Although I can't say I'm surprised.' But, after she met her South African, everything changed. She gave up the bright lights, instead squirreling away her salary until she had enough money for the fare out to South Africa. One family event that might have decided her to seize the day and try a new life away from England was the death of her brother James on 12 September 1955 aged just 42.

For Russell Endean, meanwhile, it was once again back in the old routine, weekdays working at the United Building Society, while at weekends he continued playing for Old Johannians, and for Transvaal in the Currie Cup competition, but with the added joy of writing and receiving frequent intimate airmail letters to and from London WC6. Not surprisingly for a man who had at last found his 'Miss Right', he had an outstanding summer: he was the leading run-scorer in the 1955/6 South African first-class season, scoring 591 runs at 59.1. During the summer he played a number of outstanding innings: against Eastern Province at Ellis Park he made 247 in 287 minutes, 'I won't worry if I never see a better innings, for this was majestic batting,' wrote Eric Litchfield in the *Johannesburg Sunday Times*. 'The majority of his runs came from powerful, beautifully-timed drives through the cover field, and when really flogging the bowling in the mid-afternoon he swept McKinnon over the mid-wicket pickets.' And in another out-of-character innings, in a losing cause against Western Province at Newlands – chasing 272 to win in four hours he made 91 not out, his last fifty coming in twenty-seven minutes. On Christmas Eve at Kingsmead, Durban against the powerful Natal bowling attack that included Adcock, Heine and David Ironside, he made 136, this time in more characteristic 'Endless' fashion, occupying the crease for six hours and twelve minutes. Adventurously led by all-rounder Clive van Ryneveld, the unfancied Western Province team won the Currie Cup, although in the final match of the season Transvaal, who eventually finished third, could have captured the title if they had won the match outright against the eventual winners. But in a low-scoring match on a rain-affected pitch, Western Province scraped home by two wickets.

By the autumn of 1956 Muriel Tredwell had saved her fare to South Africa, and had decided with Maureen Howell – a close friend at work – that they would leave H.S.A. & Campbell, book one-way tickets and sail to Cape Town. For Muriel and the ever-cautious Russell, it was a chance to get to know each other better. For Maureen it was simply a great big adventure. The two young English women moved into a Johannesburg apartment at Wonder Heights on Claim Street Hillbrow, a few miles south from where the Endean family lived in Crawford Avenue, Waverley. This was an era when well-educated English secretaries were in demand throughout the world and Muriel quickly landed a job in the Johannesburg offices of the giant airline Pan American World Airways Inc. She worked as the PA to Paddy Bell, a pocket-dynamo Irish-American who combined his job as an executive of the South African arm of Pan Am with his role as a popular fruity-voiced broadcaster on commercial radio. Muriel quickly made friends at work and, during weekends and holidays when Russell was playing cricket, she donned shorts and a sun hat and explored her new surroundings: camping on game reserves; watching displays of native gum-boot dancing; and visiting the Voortrekker Monument outside Pretoria where one day a year the sun's rays shine on a stone inscribed with the words 'We For Thee South Africa'.

Muriel and Shirley, a Pan Am friend, exploring South Africa, 1956

Muriel Tredwell had sailed into South Africa just prior to Peter May's 1956/7 MCC team. Fresh from their home series victory over the Australians, the England team could justifiably claim to be cricket's number-one side in Test cricket. The five-match series in South Africa became a chance for the Springboks (still smarting from the 1955 umpiring injustices) to knock the visitors off their perch. Jack Cheetham, because of business commitments, was not available to captain so Jackie McGlew – a successful vice-captain in England – was the obvious replacement. But through a complicated combination of injuries he only played once in the series, and it was Western Province captain Clive van Ryneveld who skippered for the other four Tests. Despite his relatively poor form on the 1955 England tour, Russell Endean was still considered one of the core components of the Springboks team, and his impressive form with the bat the previous summer had assured his place in the team.

The series turned out to be fiercely contested and at times controversial. England carried all before them in the early provincial matches – beating Western Province, Eastern Province, Orange Free State, Rhodesia twice and Transvaal (Endean made 81), with captain Peter May scoring 717 runs, including five centuries. On the day before the Transvaal game, emphasising the amateur status of the local cricketers, *The Star* published a photograph of two of the team, Endean and Gerald Ritchie, at their Johannesburg day jobs. Ritchie, who worked in a sports goods store, is showing an elderly gentleman the latest line in tennis racquets; while Russell – in a white shirt and spotted tie – is seen with a colleague poring over some gigantic ledgers. The caption

MCC players in early tour practice at Cape Town

reads: 'Tomorrow they face the cricket might of the MCC, but today it was simply business as usual for the Transvaal "week-end" cricketers.'

Starting on Christmas Eve, England dominated the first Test in Johannesburg on the cavernous New Wanderers Ground, winning by 171 runs. The first day set the tone for the series, England finishing on 147-3 with opener Peter Richardson, after six hours batting, having crawled to 69 not out. The Worcestershire opener tells the story of how that evening he and Alan Oakman were in a group at a drinks party where a lady remarked, 'I do hope that man who batted all day is more fun socially than he is on the field.' The blushing batsman said he kept his head down while 'Oakman left immediately, he couldn't wait to tell everybody.' Next day Richardson was finally dismissed for 117, he had taken eight hours and ten minutes to reach his hundred – at the time the slowest century in Test history. England totalled 268. South Africa then ground out 215, Goddard top-scoring with 49 and Statham, Bailey and Wardle taking three wickets each. England on a wearing pitch made only 150 but then dismissed South Africa for 72, with Bailey 5-20 the main destroyer; May (6 &14) and Endean (18 & 3) failing in both innings. The match included a highly charged incident, only recalled by Doug Insole some 60 years later. The Essex batsman was at the non-striker's end when Denis Compton hit an uppish straight drive back to the bowler Hugh Tayfield. He scooped up the ball and claimed the catch. Compton, looking hard at Tayfield, asked him if he had caught it; having been assured that he did, the England number three unhesitatingly began to walk off. Insole however was convinced it had not carried and called out: 'Denis, ask the umpire.' To which Compton replied: 'He says he caught it, that's fine.' As he headed towards the pavilion, Endean – offended by this blatant cheating – said: 'Denis, why don't you ask the umpire?' But the Middlesex man had accepted the bowler's word, so kept on walking. Insole maintains that newsreel film of the catch was never broadcast because it clearly showed that the ball had pitched two feet in front of the bowler.

The second Test in Cape Town started on New Year's Day 1957. Among the festive crowd sitting in the segregated section would have been a talented young 'Cape Coloured' cricketer, Basil D'Oliveira – who, according to Peter Oborne, 'from his vantage point in the Cage at Newlands, cheered on May, Insole and Cowdrey'. But Clive van Ryneveld, in his autobiography *20th Century All-Rounder*, disputes the existence of the Cage: 'It was not like that at Newlands. The south-western corner of the ground was a good viewing area closer to the pitch than virtually any other viewing area, and it was not enclosed by a fence.' Thanks to a solid all-round batting performance, with Cowdrey's 101 the outstanding contribution, the visitors posted 369. South Africa – with McGlew captain despite not being fit – replied with 205, Waite top-scoring with 49; the out-of-form Endean, batting at number eight, was bowled by Johnny Wardle for 17. The outstanding performance for England was the bowling of the Yorkshire spinner who took 12 wickets in the match (5-53 & 7-36). 'They couldn't read him,' recalled *The Times*'s John Woodcock. 'He tormented them.' Wardle bowled exclusively out of the back of the hand with a well-disguised googly that the Springboks batsmen just could not spot. 'Well, the pitches were perfect for me,' he himself remembered in a later TV interview. 'One: there was a little bit of bounce in them; two: Goddard bowled over the wicket for South Africa and roughed it up a little bit outside the off-stump; and three, at Newlands there was a cross-wind blowing that drifted the ball to off, and the chinaman turned from off to leg, and it was devastating when that breeze used to drift it one way, and the spin took it back the other.' Doug Insole said that for all those who witnessed it, 'it was the best display of spin-bowling they'd ever seen.' England were able to declare their second innings on 220 for 6 and, although at first the cautious May tried unsuccessfully to persuade Wardle to bowl finger spin, the Springboks were out for the same total, 72 – that they had collapsed to in the second innings in Johannesburg. Russell Endean, back at number four, got into such a muddle facing Wardle that, after the ball had looped up off his pad, he palmed the ball away before it landed on the stumps and was dismissed 'handled the ball' for 3. Afterwards he was completely at a loss as to why he had done it. Clive van Ryneveld's thought was that his hockey instincts might have taken over when he tried to bring the ball under control. Some years later Endean – true to character – said, 'I thought of heading it away but that seemed too theatrical.'

2nd Test: Endean out 'Handled Ball'

2nd Test: May fails again, caught Waite bowled Tayfield 8

The Cape Town victory by 312 runs meant that England were two up in the series and, for the Springboks, the third Test in Durban became a crunch match. Peter May won his third toss in a row (van Ryneveld was back captaining the Springboks) and chose to bat first. After an opening partnership of 115 between Trevor Bailey and the left-hander Peter Richardson, who scored a surprisingly fluent 68 on a slow lifeless Kingsmead pitch, England finished the day on 184-4 with Bailey 71 not out. During this agonisingly slow day, the Durban-born Tayfield bowled 14 consecutive maidens (extended next morning to a world-record 137 scoreless deliveries). Nine of the maidens were bowled to Bailey, who played forward to every ball regardless of length. The poet Alan Ross in *Cape Summer*, his evocative book of the tour, mused that the 'hypnotic maiden had become as soothing and necessary to Bailey as opium to a mandarin.'

On the second day England buckled to 218. South Africa eventually made 283 thanks to exactly 100 from an unusually restrained Roy McLean. Wardle was England's most successful bowler taking 5-61. Once again May who scored just 2, and Endean with 5, had failed in their sides' first innings. The tourists' second innings that was going well at 167-4, folded in the face of a quite outstanding sustained spell of off-spin bowling by 'Toey' Tayfield (he toed the ground before he bowled). On his 28th birthday he finished with 8-69 (off 37.7 overs): the best innings figures by a South African, beating Sibley Snooke's 8-70 against England in 1905/6. Because of earlier incidents on the tour, Doug Insole had not taken to Tayfield. 'I didn't like him as a man, so I was determined not to get out to him,' the Essex man told the author in 2015. 'I fancied him, he was made for the lap shot – I put my front foot in front of middle stump, and gave him the heave-ho. During the tour I scored a lot of runs off him.' Insole made 110 in England's second innings, reaching his century with last man Statham at the other end. The pundits had questioned the selection of the Cambridge blue – they had thought his inelegant and unfashionable leg-side play unsuited to Test cricket – but the unflappable Insole proved his critics wrong, finishing the low scoring, five-match series with the most runs (319) and top of the England averages at 39. During the four and a half hours left for play of this third Test, neither side was prepared to go for the win. Chasing 190, South Africa found themselves at one time at 49-4 so shut up shop, at which there was none better than Endean who made 26 in two and a half hours to deny England, the Springboks finishing at close of play on 142-6. His long stay at the crease on the final day had helped Endean to find some much needed form; in a drawn game against Rhodesia immediately after the Test he hit 171 in Transvaal's first innings, sharing in a third-wicket partnership of 218 with Ken Funston.

Despite the animosity between Insole and Tayfield and the unremitting hostility of fast bowlers Adcock and Heine – sometimes more interested in pinning batsmen than taking wickets – the relationship between the two sides was friendly. Denis and Valerie Compton threw a wild party for the players and the press corps at their Isipingo home on the Saturday night of the third Test. Denis of all the England players was the most popular with South Africans – he was admired by men, hero-worshipped by children and lusted over by women. But, as Peter Richardson remembered in 2005, Compton could never say 'no' to an invitation, and often said 'yes' to two or three parties on the same evening, which somewhat tarnished his reputation. The Worcestershire amateur, in another behind-the-scenes tale, said that in these more relaxed times it was Peter May rather than manager Freddie Brown who made sure that some early-night discipline was exercised during the Tests, 'Fred didn't in case he wasn't there himself. Fred was more likely to be meeting the Dewar's [scotch whisky] representative with a case of, which always went in to the manager's bedroom.'

The draw in Durban meant the series was still open, but a win for South Africa was vital. The stand-in Springboks captain Clive van Ryneveld, cut short his honeymoon at Plettenberg Bay so he could travel north to be ready for the start of the Fourth Test. Meanwhile his new bride Verity was flown up to Johannesburg at the expense of the South African Cricket Association but frustratingly they would not allow her to stay in the team's hotel. Van Ryneveld won his first toss as a married man, and chose to bat on a grassless pitch. Only a few hundred spectators were scattered amongst the tiers of backless wooden benches that circled the New Wanderers stadium, the vast bowl that had replaced the old ground. Locals had stayed away because the Springboks were two down, on top of which the batting by both sides in the series had been dreadfully laboured. At the end of the first day of this do-or-die encounter, the home side's top-order had made reasonable progress, on 234 for 4 at close of play. On the second day, a Saturday, an expectant 30,000 crowd turned up to see the Springboks accumulate a match-winning total and for McLean (53 not out at the start of play) to score a century. But they were disappointed: South Africa made no more than a decent total of 340, and McLean, after a mix up with his skipper, was run out for 93. Russell Endean, batting at number seven, was bowled by Statham for 13. England in their first innings made a below par 251; May (batting without a cap for the first time in the Tests) scored 61, his only decent innings in a series in which he averaged just 15.3. England's disappointing reply was down to Tayfield: in another marathon spell – 37 overs, fifteen of them maidens – he took 4-79. South Africa then squandered their strong position by being dismissed for 142. There were three wickets for Statham and two each for Bailey and Wardle; Endean, with yet another failure, made 2. England had seven hours to score the 231 needed to win the game and the series; and at one point with their score at 147 for 2, it looked as though

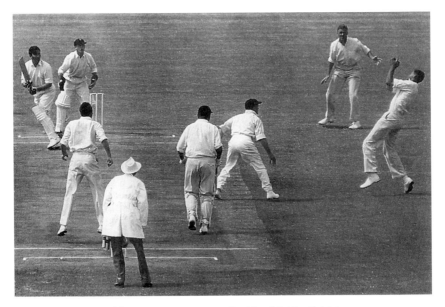

4th Test: Compton, ct Goddard b Tayfield 1

they would do it. But with an extraordinary, day-long spell of bowling, Tayfield gradually wore down the visitors' batting and England were dismissed for 214. The off spinner finished with the still record Test figures for a South African of 9-113. When brother Arthur Tayfield (on as a sub) caught the last man Peter Loader on the boundary, an ecstatic crowd swarmed on to the field and carried Hugh Tayfield and Clive van Ryneveld shoulder-high to the pavilion. But not all the crowd were cheering: octogenarian Maureen Taylor, who went to this Test with her friend Muriel Tredwell, recalled that 'most of the seats were for whites and a separate section for blacks. The blacks rooted for the visiting team.'

After such a memorable fourth Test, the final match of the series reverted to type and was another dour affair. Played on a recently re-laid pitch at St George's Park, Port Elizabeth, there was already a mosaic of inch-wide cracks in the strip before the start of play. England were weakened because Wardle (whose cartilage had slipped out while he was playing snooker) and Statham, who had taken 40 victims between them in the series, were both unavailable and were replaced by Tyson and Lock. The all-important toss – that virtually decided the match – was won by van Ryneveld, who remembered that 'when the ball hit those cracks it did unpredictable things, mainly shoot along the ground, but also deviate.' On the first day the heavily watered pitch was at its best, but even so South Africa only managed 138 for 5. On day two, with every other ball a shooter, the Springboks were quickly dismissed for 164; top scorer was Endean, batting for four hours, forty-eight minutes for an invaluable 70 (no other batsman made a fifty in the match). 'When we batted the ball didn't rise more than a foot, and at the end, two inches,' was how Peter Richardson describes the pitch, 'It was hopeless for me who was a back-foot player. Perfect for Trevor [Bailey] with the old forward defence prod – he was there for hours. Oh they hated him, and he loved it.'

In a stay of nearly two and a half hours, Bailey top-scored with 41 in England's total of 110. In their second innings South Africa scraped together 134; Frank Tyson, with Godfrey Evans standing up to the stumps as the ball was keeping so low, took 6-40. England had no realistic chance of scoring the 189 for victory, and it was only thanks to some desperate tail-end hitting from Evans, Lock and Tyson which doubled the score, that they managed 130, Hugh Tayfield finishing with the relatively expensive return of 6-78. In the drawn five-match series in which the ball dominated the bat (the average scoring rate was 32 runs an hour), Tayfield took 37 wickets at 17.18 – a South African record for most wickets in a series, which still stands to the present day. This was the apex of the great Springbok's Test career; as was the series for Yorkshire spinner Johnny Wardle, whose return was 26 wickets at 13.8 in his four Tests. This final match at Port Elizabeth proved to be Denis Compton's Test swansong. His illustrious career that spanned more than two decades had brought great joy to many thousands around the globe. 'He played with such great charm you know; he played not as though he was a professional but as though he was an amateur enjoying himself,' reminisced John Woodcock sitting in his sunny Longparish walled garden in 2009. 'If I had to see one batsman again in my life play an innings at the top of his form, I think it would be Denis.'

With the series over and Russell Endean having at last made a contribution to South Africa's fight back – as well as his runs, he also kept wicket in England's second innings, taking fine catches to dismiss Compton and Evans – he could now concentrate on other more life-changing events. He was convinced (as was Muriel) that they were made for each other, and on the 21 July 1957 news of their engagement was announced in the national newspapers. The strap line to the *Johannesburg Sunday Times*'s photograph of the beaming, not-so-young couple – he was 33, she was 29 – taken in the Pan Am office in front of a picture of the New York skyline read: 'SA Cricket's "Confirmed Bachelor" to wed'. Whether Russell's betrothal broke the hearts of any locals is hard to say, but Jane Lawther, daughter of one of his closest school friends, remembers that 'everybody was shocked' when he chose an English woman. The marriage was planned to take place on 7 September 1957 (like all sensible cricketers, Russell had arranged the marriage out of the cricket season). Once the date was set, Muriel wrote to the Population Registrar to apply for a government-issued Identity Card, an essential document for all those planning to live permanently in apartheid South Africa. Russell's parents made the wedding arrangements: the ceremony was held at St Martin's-in-the-Veld, the Anglican church in Rosebank; and the reception in the Palm Court room at the Old Johannians Club. 'Muriel made a golden bride with her beautiful blonde hair covered by a tiny veil and simple coronet,' effused 'Katherine' in the *Old Johannian*. 'Her lovely ballet-length gown with tight waist, long sleeves and full skirt was of cream satin, brocaded in dull gold, and she carried one large orchid.' Her boss, Paddy Bell, gave the bride away and Maureen Howell, the London friend who had joined her in Johannesburg, was the only bridesmaid. Sadly, Muriel's mother, now living in a brand new council flat in Clem Attlee Court, Lillie Road, Fulham, could not afford the fare to see her daughter being married, sending instead a touching telegram, 'My blessing and wishes for your happiness. Love Mummy.' Of the many messages waiting for the newly weds at the reception, the most predictable sent by Old Johannians cricket members read: 'At last you've bowled a maiden over.' After former Springboks captain Jack Cheetham had toasted the parents, and Paddy Bell had given a typically witty speech to toast the bride and groom, the guests waited with some trepidation as the normally less than loquacious bridegroom rose to reply. But he surprised them all with a charmingly assured response;

his astonished father, Bill observing that his son said more in his speech than he usually did 'in a week at home'.

Numerous stories and photographs of the event appeared in the Johannesburg newspapers: in one picture, John Waite kisses the bride; in another, while a smiling Neil Adcock looks on, a serious-looking Hugh Tayfield (who would be five-times married) gives Russell a cautionary hand shake. The journalists almost exclusively concentrated on a 'fall of the most eligible bachelor' theme: 'Endean Eindelik Geboul' (Endean Eventually Bowled) was the headline in the Afrikaans *Die Vaderland*. But the *Rand Daily Mail* had a different take on the union, suggesting it was not cricket that drew the couple together, as Muriel's interests were 'painting, tennis and reading'. In the family archive as well as the 'Volledige Huweliksertifikaat' (Full Marriage Certificate), there is an Antenuptial Contract signed by Muriel and Russell two weeks before the marriage in the presence of Notary Public, P.C. Thompson – a document that formally designated joint ownership of the couple's assets – the honourable husband was determined to protect the interests of the woman who had travelled 5,000 miles to marry him.

21 July 1957
left to right: Neil Adcock, Hugh Tayfield, Russell
Endean, Muriel Endean, John Waite, Paddy Bell

Chapter Six

I Persuaded Russell

The honeymoon was spent in Britain, where they had flown from Johannesburg in luxury as the honoured guests of Pan Am. On the trip, as well as enjoying a glorious late English summer, they fitted in some concerts and West End shows – including snapping up tickets for the hottest theatrical event of the year – John Osborne's play *The Entertainer* starring Laurence Olivier as a seedy music hall comedian. Mollie Panter-Downes in her 'Letter From London' in The *New Yorker* said: 'It is, indeed, an extremely poor play, which will probably run and run.' But Kenneth Tynan, the *Observer*'s young theatre critic, had an alternative take: 'Mr. Osborne has had the big and brilliant notion of putting the whole of contemporary England onto one and the same stage.' On a trip to Blackpool they saw the beach-front illuminations and tasted another side of what the British stage had to offer, visiting the Opera House to see *The Big Show of 1957* starring comedy double-act, Jewel and Warriss, and the Essex-born, glamorously busty singer, Yana (Pamela Guard), who according to George Formby's biographer David Bret was famous for her fish-tail dresses and 'huge gay following'.

Most important for Muriel during their time in England was her chance to show off her handsome husband to her many London friends and to the extended Tredwell family. One of Russell's new relations was his brother-in-law Cecil, who had been a prominent footballer and cricketer, playing for Middlesex 2nd XI before the war. Now president of his local club, Malden Wanderers, he persuaded his sister to let her new spouse play for the club in an end-of-season game against local rivals Spencer at their Earlsfield ground (an area of South London that in the twenty-first century is populated by many émigré South Africans). In the match in which Russell saw the visitors home with a stylish 71, he also took what the Wanderers schoolboy wicket-keeper David Lodge remembered as the best catch he had ever seen: 'Harry Edney bowled a long hop to left handed Reg Perrell who, though no batsman, middled a full-blooded pull towards the three-man leg-trap. The other two [short-legs] were flat on the deck by then, but Endean caught it two-handed straight between his eyes about four yards from the bat.' Although all the club players were privileged to have played with a current Test player, in the bar after the match, Russell, generous as always, was quick to compliment his temporary team-mates on their high quality slip catching.

There was a welcoming party of press photographers at Jan Smuts International Airport in October when the newly-weds arrived back in Johannesburg; one snapper's shot captures them descending from the sleek

Pan Am Clipper Pathfinder. The couple had managed to find a second-floor apartment at No. 9 Marina Court, Soper Road in the city's northern district of Berea – there is a black-and-white family photograph of Muriel standing on the balcony showing off her 'new cotton tiered-skirt'. She returned to work at Pan

Muriel Endean standing on the balcony of the new Johannesburg apartment

Am, and Russell resumed his duties as a district auditor for the Union Building Society. He missed some of the 1957/8 season's early games for Transvaal but played regularly for Old Johannians at weekends, and was picked for the provincial game against the visiting Australians. In a match in which the tourists thrashed the home side, Endean made a stubborn 60 in his side's first innings which ensured him a place in the Springboks' team for the first Test. South Africa, having more than held their own against both Australia and England in recent years, were considered to have a very good chance of winning the forthcoming series. Without the likes of Lindwall, Miller and Hassett, the young and inexperienced visitors – the local press describing them as the weakest team ever to visit the Union – were captained by the balding twenty-two-year-old pharmacist, Ian Craig. South Africa selected as their captain for the series Clive van Ryneveld, who had recently been elected as a United Party MP for the East London constituency. But in November 1959, along with Helen Suzman, he joined a small group that broke away to form the Progressive Party that opposed the ever-tightening apartheid laws of the ruling National Party.

The two captains: Ian Craig and Clive van Ryneveld

The result of the first Test that started at the New Wanderers Ground on 23 December 1957 suggested that it would be a close series. The match started in bitterly cold weather, with South Africa, on a hard, true surface, batting slowly but steadily all day for 220-2. Progress was slightly better on day two, the Springboks declaring half an hour before the close for 470-9 (McGlew scoring 108, Waite 115, Goddard 90, and Endean and McLean both making exactly 50). Australia's most successful bowler was Ian Meckiff (5-125) the left-arm quickie with the huge drag – his front foot landing a good foot in front of the popping crease. Coupled with bowling off about eighteen yards, he also had a very suspect action. Australia, in danger of following on at 150-5, were saved by a barnstorming innings from their number seven, Richie Benaud. His quick-fire 122 thrilled the record Boxing Day crowd of 36,057and raised the visitors' total to 368. Collapsing to 19-4 in their second innings, South Africa were in danger of losing the match until rescued by Endean and Waite who, on a still lightning-fast Wanderers pitch, fended off the hostile bowling of Meckiff and Davidson for three-hours. Their dogged 129-run partnership broke the South African 5th wicket record. Waite made 59, while Endean, who according to Louis Duffus 'was prepared to play good-length bowling until doomsday,' batted for over four-hours for his 77. The Springboks eventually crawled to 201 (Davidson 6-34, Meckiff 3-52). The home side were slowed down mid-innings by a spell of defensive bowling by off-spinner Jimmy Burke that upset Waite. 'He was a blatant thrower. There was no way he should have been allowed to bowl in any Test cricket.' During Burke's spell the crowd had started to protest about his action, but after conferring the umpires allowed him to carry on bowling. Nearly 20,000 turned up in anticipation of a close fifth-day finish – the press had predicted that Hugh Tayfield would be the match-winner – but, as they were to do for the whole series, the Australian batsmen, with judicious use of their feet, were able to nullify the off-spinner, the match petering out to a tame draw – Australia finishing on 162-3. South Africa, as in the previous summer's series against England, had been unable to score fast enough to set up the realistic chance of a win; but for Endean it had been an excellent match. '[He] had shown his willingness to hit the loose ball powerfully,' was Roy McLean's assessment in his book of the series, *Sackcloth Without Ashes*. 'It was not always thus. He is a much better batsman when not coiled up into entire defence, an attractive player when the springs are let loose.'

By the time the second Test was under way in Cape Town, the Tredwell family in London had received news that Muriel was pregnant and that the Endeans were expecting their first child in June. Craig won the all-important toss at Newlands and Australia, thanks to 189 from Burke, made 449. South Africa replied with a disappointing 209 in the first innings and, following on, could only manage an even more disappointing 99; chinaman-and-googly bowler Lindsay Kline finishing the match with a hat-trick. As they had done in the Cape Town Test a year earlier, the Springboks' batsmen were unable to cope with the turning ball that drifted in the strong south-easterly blowing off the ocean. In 1957 it was left-arm wrist-spinner Wardle who bowled them out twice; twelve months later, Richie Benaud, with match figures of 9-144, was the back-of-the-hand destroyer. 'It was round about the time I'd learnt to bowl the flipper,' recalled Benaud. 'It was just a little addition to the repertoire that came in handy.' The expectant father, who in the first innings had made a patient 21 before being thrown out by 'chucker' Burke, was, in the second innings comprehensively bowled for five, playing back to a Benaud googly (or was it a flipper?) that fizzed past his bat before knocking back the middle stump.

The third Test at Kingsmead, Durban was described by Benaud as 'one of the most boring games of cricket in which I have played at paddock, school, club, first-class or Test level'. This was the match in which Jackie McGlew (batting for 545 minutes) broke the year-old record set by Peter Richardson (488 minutes) of the slowest century in Test history. After Australia in their first innings had been bowled out on a lively pitch for 163 (Neil Adcock 6-43), South Africa then took thirteen hours and five minutes to score 384 (Endean caught Simpson bowled Benaud 15). In the day and a half left, Australia fairly comfortably played out time, finishing on 292 for 7, ensuring that the match subsided into the drabbest-of-drab draws.

South Africa fell to ignominious defeat in the last two Tests. At the New Wanderers Stadium, Johannesburg they lost by ten wickets; and at St George's Park, Port Elizabeth Australia won by eight wickets. The difference between the two sides, apart from the growing confidence of a winning team, was the presence of two outstanding New South Walean all-rounders, Alan Davidson and Richie Benaud, both at the height of their powers. In the fourth Test Benaud, batting at number four, made exactly 100; Davidson, who came in at number nine, scored a bludgeoning 62 in the Australians' total of 401. Writing about this match, Benaud made much of Adcock and Heine's hostile bowling and the 'fire of the verbal exchanges', which the leg-spinner, with choir-boy innocence, said 'were all one-way traffic.' South Africa made 203 and, following on, only 198 in their second innings, leaving the visitors just one run for victory. Benaud had taken 9-154 in the match to go with his century. Opening the batting in this game, Russell Endean did not have such a bad match: he was lbw to Davidson in the first innings for 22; and, after a three-hour stay at the crease in the Springboks' second innings, made 38 before being caught by Simpson at slip from a sharply-turning Benaud leg-break.

South Africa chose to bat first in the final Test on a green St George's' pitch, and having been 105-7, did well to scramble to 214 all out by close of play. The recovery was thanks to Hugh Tayfield who, as well as making 66, shepherded the nineteen-year-old Peter Carlstein through to a hard-fought 32. Australia's first innings total of 291 (Mackay 77 not out, McDonald 58 and Benaud 43) gave them a lead of 77 which they consolidated by dismissing South Africa for 144 in the second innings (Davidson 5-38, Benaud 5-82); and, despite a barrage of bumpers (53 in 56 balls) from Adcock and Heine, the win was achieved for the loss of two wickets. In what was a friendly series, gentlemanly conducted by Ian Craig and Clive van Ryneveld, the Springboks captain took his two angry fast bowlers off after they had refused to cut out the short stuff. For Endean, dismissed twice by Davidson for 2 and 23, it had been an undistinguished match with the bat, but the *Rand Daily Mail* reported that at the age of thirty-three he showed that he had lost none of his skills as one of the world's best fielders. On the second day, one of 'Endean's famous catches low-down at full stretch' dismissed Burke. On day three, standing at straight silly-mid-on to Tayfield, he caught Craig off a fiercely struck on-drive. Earlier in the day he had taken a 'wonder catch' to dismiss Grout. There is good black-and-white film of this dismissal – Endean, fielding at very fine leg-slip, flings himself to his left and grabs a one-handed catch off a genuine leg-glance.

The local newsreel footage of the series shows Test cricket that looks surprisingly modern in most respects: the fast bowlers are coming in off long runs; there are plenty of bouncers, and the keepers are standing well back. The catching is often spectacular, while the out-fielding is athletically committed, and the throwing powerful from the boundary edge. The batsmen bravely (often bareheaded) get behind the short-pitched bowling, and even though the scoring rates are slow, they play a wide variety of back and front-foot shots. When it comes to appealing and celebrating, the players do not hold back (the restrained Endean being an exception). Heine, Adcock and Benaud are uninhibited – the Aussie leg-spinner in one lbw shout is down on one knee with arms above his head, flamboyantly pleading with the umpire. He got the decision.

In this final Test, as has had been the case throughout the series, the difference between the two sides was the dominance of Australia's two bowling all-rounders, Benaud and Davidson. In this last match the powerful left-arm seamer took 9-82; while the debonair leg-spinner returned figures of 6-116. The left-arm wrist-spinner Lindsay Kline – who although overshadowed by Benaud, topped the series averages with 15 wickets at 16.3 – came up with an explanation as to why the Springboks batsmen had been so comprehensively undone by the Australian attack. He thought that Davidson, Benaud, Meckiff and he himself found so many outside edges because they all mostly took the ball away from the South African right-handers; and in this series the record of the slip fielders – Robert ('Bobby' came later) Simpson with 13 catches; Benaud with 5; and keeper Grout with 16 grabs – suggests that Kline's theory holds water.

During the last game of the tour against South African Universities (a drawn match which Benaud described in his autobiography as an 'easy' victory), the leg-spinner captured four final wickets, which took his tour total in an exhausting 742.7 overs to 106 at 19.39 (he also scored 817 runs at 51.06), This beat the previous record of 104 wickets on a South African tour held by England's Sydney Barnes who bowled just 336 overs with an average of 10.74 per wicket on the 1913/4 MCC tour.

****

Just over three months after the Australians left South Africa, on 29 June 1958, at the local State hospital, Muriel gave birth to Mark, a nine-pound boy named after her deceased father. Now a public figure, a picture with her new-born son made all the national newspapers; and pasted in the family scrapbook is a cutting from the Afrikaans newspaper *Die Vaderland* with the heading, 'Krieketheld se Eerste' (Cricket Hero's First). Russell has added a handwritten translation of the picture's caption: 'Mrs Endean, the attractive wife of Russell Endean, the well known Springbok cricketer, gave birth on Sunday morning to a lovely son at a Johannesburg maternity hospital. This is her first-born.' The journalist went on to quote from his interview with the new mother: '"A big boy" she said this morning. "Will he also be a cricketer? That's a question. I hope so but I think it's a little too early too say,"' Mark Russell Endean was baptised on 21 September at St Martin-in-the-Veld where a year earlier his parents had been married. In December Muriel posted to her mother in England a happy black-and-white photograph of Russell holding son Mark aged six months; on the back of which she has written: 'Doesn't he look grown up now? Who is he like? His hair is fair.' The new family of three spent Christmas Day 1958 with Russell's parents, and his older brother Howard, his wife and their two sons. Howard Endean, after serving with distinction in the Second World War, went back to England to study at the College of Aeronautics before establishing himself in South Africa as a noted engineer and inventor. Amongst other things he designed a tennis-racquet press that stopped the wooden frame from warping; and built the first single-seat, ultralight aircraft, the Druin D31 Turbulent, in South Africa.

The day after the Christmas Day family celebrations, Russell was playing in the first day of a Currie Cup match game against Natal at the New Wanderers ground. He made only 6 and 14 in a low-scoring match won by the home side. Although Transvaal were Currie Cup winners, for Endean personally

*Mark Endean's first Christmas alongside Russell's mother
and his brother Howard's family*

the 1958/9 season was uneventful. Due to work commitments and parental duties, he appeared only four times for Transvaal. In seven innings he scored 171 runs with an average of 24.42. On a damp pitch he played a masterly defensive innings of 53 at Salisbury in the drawn game against Rhodesia; and at the Wanderers in the return match (also drawn) he made 56 – his best score of the season. Playing for Rhodesia was the twenty-year-old Colin Bland who would make his name as a transformative fielder – one of the best the game has ever seen.

The 1959/60 season saw Russell Endean back to his best; but Transvaal surrendered their hold on the Currie Cup, finishing runner-up to Natal. In a summer of high scores – Sid O'Linn, the Charlton Athletic footballer, topped the averages with 619 runs at 68.77 and the by now thirty-five-year-old veteran Endean was fifth (504 runs at 50.4). His most notable innings was 204 not out against Border. On 96 at the end of day one, next day he scored another 108 before lunch – the second time in his career he scored a hundred in a morning session. 'We just didn't know how we going to get him out,' recalled Robin Thorne, Border's opening bowler, speaking from his Berkshire home in 2016. 'He had all the shots and everything was hitting the middle of the bat.' Transvaal declared on 397-2 (Thorne 30-9-80-1) and went on to win by an innings and 44 runs. Border, who had been promoted from B Section of the Currie Cup, were generally out of their depth in the higher division; in a match against Natal in East London they lost by 350 runs, being dismissed for 16 (Goddard 6-3) and 18 (Griffin 7-11), still the lowest two-innings total in first-class cricket. Against much stronger opposition in Bulawayo, Endean scored a patient 117 not out in Transvaal's victory over Rhodesia. In his last first-class game of the season against Natal, he was twice clean-bowled by Geoff Griffin (another fast bowler with a suspect action) for 0 and 7. Some years later he remembered the difficulty of facing 'chuckers', particularly Ian Meckiff: 'It was not so much the sighting of the ball,' he said, 'but in adjusting to the unusual trajectory and unnatural pace.'

The season was also notable for two short October tours: a powerful Commonwealth team led by Denis Compton that played five games in Transvaal; and a Surrey CCC side which visited Rhodesia. The men from the Oval had been invited as the team who had been county champions seven times in a row in the 1950s. Their leisurely three-week tour included, as well as two three-day games, some golf, and a three-day trip to the spectacular Victoria Falls. In the first match at the Police Ground, Salisbury – where Surrey's unwell number eleven, Peter Loader, to the annoyance of his team-mates, refused to bat – they were beaten by two runs by a strong Rhodesia side that included in their eleven a Duckworth and a Lewis. In the second match in Bulawayo, the twenty-two-year-old John Edrich scored a match-saving 151 in Surrey's second innings. The stand-out player for the home side in the two matches was the discarded Springboks' Test player Percy Mansell; the Telford-born all-rounder scored 118 in three innings and took 19 wickets for 278 with his leg-spinners. Russell Endean played against the Commonwealth team in only one of their three first-class fixtures during their short tour. He scored 30 and 19 for the Combined Transvaal XI, being bowled by Compton in his second innings, as the tourists won a closely fought game by three wickets. Chasing 242 in 195 minutes, thanks mainly to an elegant 100 not out in 137 minutes by Tom Graveney, they got home with five minutes to spare. Revelling on the fast and true Transvaal tracks, in his five innings the Gloucestershire batsman made 343 runs, with an average of 114.33.

Despite being a dedicated father and loving husband, Endean's weekly routine had not changed a great deal – it was still the office from Monday to Friday, with regular trips around the country to audit the books of branch offices of the United Building Company, while at weekends he continued to play club cricket, and took annual leave to represent Transvaal in the Currie Cup. But for Muriel, life after giving birth had changed dramatically – her work and friends in the stimulating environment of the Pan Am office were things of the past; she was now a new mother with a small baby living in a quiet suburb away from the excitement of the city. She was also without the support of her own mother, over 5,000 miles away; something she particularly needed since there was some friction in the relationship with her mother-in-law. Weekends she would make her way to the clubby, male-dominated world of Old Johannians Sports Club where she could at least share her worries and experiences with other young mothers. But after three years of life in this foreign land, seeds of discontent were beginning to ferment.

At the beginning of 1960 Muriel, a keen (left-of-centre) follower of politics, would have been aware of the visit of the British Prime Minister, Harold Macmillan, to South Africa to mark the 50th anniversary of the Union. On 3 February he gave his 'wind of change' speech to the two Houses of Parliament in Cape Town in which, although having some warm words for the country, he emphatically condemned the apartheid system: 'Where different races or tribes live side by side, the task is to ensure that all people may enjoy security and freedom and the chance to contribute as individuals.' Clive van Ryneveld, who was present at the event and has a signed souvenir of the visit, recalls that the Union prime minister Dr Verwoerd 'in reply thanked Macmillan for visiting South Africa and said that while we shared the same ideals we did not necessarily agree on the method of achieving them.' Some six weeks later, on 21 March in Sharpeville, armed police mowed down sixty-nine people who had been among the many thousands protesting against the new pass laws. This massacre, and the ever-tightening grip of apartheid, had repercussions around the world. In England there were protests and debates about whether that summer's Springboks tour should go ahead. England amateur cricketers and former team mates at Cambridge University, Peter May and the Reverend David Sheppard, were on opposing sides of the divide – the Church of England priest saying he would not play against the tourists as long as their selection policy was to consider whites only. A year later John Waite, the Springbok's keeper on the tour published *Perchance to Bowl* (a strange title for a gloveman) that challenged Sheppard's stance. In a chapter entitled 'Why White Cricketers Do Not Play Non-White Players in South Africa', he wrote that 'the black and coloured public of South Africa is not equipped or ready for multi-racial sport any more than the black and coloured public of the Union is ready to govern South Africa or to manage its industries.' He went on to say that the unfortunates 'must prove that they can take a victory and a licking before inter-racial and multi-racial sport can safely be conducted in South Africa.'

Following his excellent season Russell Endean would have been an almost certain selection for South Africa's 1960 tour to England but, because there was a strict 'no wives' rule, he was reported as saying that he was 'unwilling to leave her [Muriel] alone in a country where she was still a comparative stranger.' And so he chose to watch from afar at what turned out to be an unhappy tour that included not only anti-apartheid demonstrations but also the Griffin throwing controversy and a three-nil drubbing for the Springboks. Endean's opinion was that it was unwise to have sent Griffin on the tour as he had already been no-balled for throwing on at least two occasions while playing for Natal.

After some hesitation, Endean made himself available for the 1960/1 Transvaal domestic season, and he played regularly for Old Johannians at weekends. There was no touring team visiting the Union, so first-class cricket was confined to the Currie Cup. Transvaal finished sixth (Transvaal B finished fourth) in a new-style competition that incorporated ten teams. He had only a moderate season, scoring 325 runs at 29.94, with his highest score of the summer being against Rhodesia on Boxing Day in front of a sweltering 20,834 Johannesburg holiday crowd. 'Russell Endean reinstated himself in Transvaal and perhaps South African cricket at the Wanderers yesterday by scoring 122 in a manner mightily reminiscent of many of the innings he played eight summers ago in Australia.' wrote Dick Whittington in the *Johannesburg Sunday Times*. 'Endean mixed patches of straight-batted brilliance with quieter periods during his 278-minute stay.'

The headline for a photograph in *The Star* on 6 March 1961 reads: 'Old Johannians – the club team of the year.' A young outfit captained by veteran Endean, won both of Johannesburg's major cricket tournaments – the Transvaal League and the Lionel Phillips competition. Also in March, Muriel was stepping up to the crease again: on Thursday 30th, at the private Hillbrow Nursing Home, she gave birth to a daughter Jane, sister to Mark.

Endean captain of Old Johannians
1960/61 double winners

Two months later on 31 May, South Africa left the British Commonwealth and became a republic. The Hendrik Verwoerd government appointed a State President (Charles Swart) to replace the Queen and her representative, the Governor-General; and, in order to counter the underground resistance organisations such as Umkhonto we Sizwe (the armed wing of the ANC), the National Party introduced draconian security measures and intensified its control of the press. These developments no doubt would have made Muriel Endean increasingly uneasy about bringing up a young family in such an oppressive society, and on 9 July the *Johannesburg Sunday Express*, ran the story with the headline: 'Endean May Settle in Britain'. 'News that Endean and his family may be leaving was "leaked" from London last week.' wrote cricket correspondent Arthur Goldman. 'When I asked Russell for his confirmation he said: "Yes it is true that we are contemplating moving overseas.'" After weighing up the options, and some wavering, Russell and Muriel did eventually make the momentous decision to up sticks and try to make a new life in England.

The news came as shock not only to close friends, but to the wider public, especially to people in the world of sport. And the story was all across the Johannesburg press, one headline read: 'I persuaded Russell, says Mrs Endean'. Elaborating on this, Muriel said 'I had always wanted to go back.' She went on to explain that the time was right now that they had two children and were looking to move from a flat to house. 'Once we bought a house [in Johannesburg] we would probably never go, so it was now or never.' While she was certain it was the right move, for Russell, to judge by what he said just before they left, there were still some doubts: 'If things did not work out in Britain, I would most probably come back to South Africa. A lot depends on whether I can find a suitable post as a chartered accountant.' By agreeing to this move he was certainly making a number of huge personal sacrifices: he had a secure, well-paid job, he was still playing first-class cricket and top-grade provincial hockey; he had the support of loving parents; and he was leaving behind a wide group of friends forged during his time at St John's College. It says much for Russell's generosity and devotion to Muriel that he was prepared to give all this up. As he also remarked: 'My wife never really settled in South Africa, the weather is one factor.' In their interviews with the press the couple had both emphasised that there were 'no political reasons for their leaving.' This was in response to the recent news that leading Springboks cricketer Trevor Goddard was leaving Durban for England with his family, specifically for 'political reasons'. In addition, another of the 1960 tourists, John Fellows Smith, had also decided to leave Durban and settle in Britain. One further South African cricketer, the 'coloured' Basil D'Oliveira, had already travelled to England the previous year. Encouraged by cricket writer John Arlott, he had gone to try his luck with Middleton CC in the Central Lancashire League.

In order to leave apartheid South Africa, Russell Endean had to purchase for two Rand (£1) a 'Vertrek' or Departure Permit. Dated 26 June 1961 and valid for five years it had to be shown to the Immigration Department on leaving and re-entry to the Union. On the document it showed that he had joint South African/British nationality, which would help smooth his entry and job seeking when he arrived in the UK. The formalities over, the Old Johannians laid on a farewell party for the family at their Linkside clubhouse. And on the last day before the family caught the train to Cape Town, Russell played one final morning game of hockey for his Old Boys 1st XI before saying an emotional goodbye to close friends at his parents' home in Waverley. On 19 July 1961 the Endean family watched the imposing outline of Table Mountain fade into the distance as the Ellerman Lines vessel the *City of Exeter* steamed out of Cape Town harbour carrying them over 5,000 miles north to an uncertain future in England. Dick Whittington, distinguished sports writer on the *Johannesburg Sunday Times* summed up what many felt in South Africa about this emblematic departure:

> Cricket on the Veld will seem a different thing next summer without the trim, springy shape of Russell Endean poised ready to pounce from his favourite springboard at leg gully upon any miracle catch that may be on the wing.
>
> Russell will be in England then, enjoying the occasional club hockey, waiting for an occasional game of club cricket when April sunshine comes.
>
> Yes, we shall miss that swallow-swift dive of his and that unusual lift of the bat as we shall miss Endean, the man, who won as much respect from his team-mates and his opponents as any cricketer of any country of any era.

Chapter Seven

Russell Sent His Bat On Ahead

The Endeans arrived in England on 3 August, and rather than heading to Fulham where Muriel's sickly mother was living, they chose to be near her brother Cecil in Surrey. Russell's arrival was a big news story, with British reporters pressing him hard as to whether it was the apartheid system that had been the reason for the family's emigration. But 'as he settled into his new home in New Malden, Surrey, last night, Endean made it clear that he is here for domestic reasons,' wrote Crawford White in the *Daily Express.* '"I am of English stock. My grandfather left Cornwall to prospect for gold in the Transvaal many years ago and my wife is a Londoner," he said. "All her family are here and we have now come with our two children to try and make our lives here."' The local paper, the *Surrey Comet,* as well as covering the Endean story, also reported in the same issue the arrival of another immigrant family: 'Polish refugees Mr and Mrs Zygmunt Kubik and their four children, who were welcomed by the mayor and mayoress of Surbiton (Councillor and Mrs DJM Greenwood), took over the home which the council had provided for them in Douglas Road.'

'Russell sent his bat on ahead,' reported the *Rand Daily Mail* on 17 July, 'but he has no definite plans for its use beyond a few club games with Malden Wanderers C.C., his brother-in-law's club.' In fact Endean was playing just two days after he landed. Although 'he didn't want to replace a regular', he went straightaway into the first team in a match against the ancient Surrey club Mitcham (founded in 1685). Agreeing to play so soon after spending eighteen days on board the *City of Exeter* proved to be a mistake – batting on sea legs, he was caught Caitlin bowled Peacock 0. This was a minor setback. In the days when serious club cricket went on until the end of September, Endean batted thirteen times for his new team, making 527 runs at 47.9. The highlight was a stylish 114 made in 122 minutes against Hastings & St Leonards Priory. This innings was compiled on the fading Victorian elegance of the Central Recreation Ground, the venue where Sussex played until 1989, after which it was concreted over to make way for a soulless shopping mall. Such pitches where first-class cricket was regularly played were more to Endean's liking than some of the softer club strips that he would bat on in the coming years.

The *Surrey Comet*, previewing the 1961 season, had announced confidently that 'Endean and Hutton will play for Malden Wanderers.' But although the former England captain, living close by on the exclusive Coombe Hill estate, did make a few appearances, it turned out to be Sir Len's two Repton schoolboy sons, Richard (Yorkshire and England) and John who became regulars for the club. During the season, Surrey and future England cricketer Micky Stewart (who had made New Malden his home) and sixteen-year-old fast bowler Geoff Arnold also turned out for the club. Arnold – restricted by Surrey coach, the former England wicket-keeper Arthur McIntyre, to ten overs a game – returned the remarkable season's figures of 50 wickets at 13.39. At an end-of-season game against Barclays Bank at their picturesque nineteenth-century Norbury ground – now sold off as a fitness centre – there is a Kodacolor photograph of Trevor Goddard and his young red-headed son watching his one-time South African teammate Endean playing for Malden Wanderers. There were hopes that the club would gain another recruit, but in 1962 the great Springbok all-rounder went north-west to play as a professional for Great Chell where, as well as taking 64 wickets at 12.15, he broke the record for most runs (1118 at 94.0) in the North Staffordshire League. After this one season in England, Goddard returned to captain South Africa on tours of Australasia and England, before, following his wife's death in 1977, becoming an assistant minister in the Pentacostal Assembly of God Church in Bellville, Cape Town.

The Britain that the Endeans arrived at in 1961 was a country that, despite the running down of the Empire, still saw itself as a top-table power that needed to maintain the prestige of sterling and its role as one of the world's policemen. 'It was almost as if, psychologically speaking, Suez had never happened,' writes David Kynaston in *A Shake of the Dice, 1959-62*, part of his epic post-war history, *Tales of a New Jerusalem*. He evokes the rapidly changing, everyday lives of the British people in the early 1960s: 'Car and television ownership were soaring, and although a pub a day was closing, sales of filter-tipped cigarettes increased sixfold between 1955 and 1960; as for alcoholic drinks, not only was Ind Coope heavily promoting Skol lager, but pubs and restaurants were increasingly willing to sell wine by the glass.' Many cinemas and dance halls were also closing or being transformed 'They changed our local Palais into a bowling alley' was a line from *Fings Aint Wot They Used T'Be*, the Lionel Bart cockney musical that wittily highlighted the growing Americanisation of British life.

The Endeans decided to make their home in the Surrey suburbs. After a brief stay in a rented flat in New Malden, they bought 1 Fullbrooks Avenue, a 1930s house in the adjoining suburb of Worcester Park, for £4,100, This mock-Tudor semi remained the family home for the next thirty-eight years. The *Surrey Comet*, as well as listing houses for sale, advertised a 1959 Morris Minor at AV Motors, Teddington for £455; while Lankester at Eden Street, Kingston offered an ('almost new') 1960 Austin A40 de lux for £635. A 19-inch black-and-white television could be rented for 9 s 4d a week; and the publicly owned GPO (a rare equal-opportunity employer) was recruiting men and women telephone operators on salaries from £8 18s 6p at 21, to £10 12s at 25 and over, rising to £12 11s a week. 'Malden and Coombe has as many as 56 different youth organisations,' noted a *Times Educational Supplement* journalist, as he lingered to take the pulse of the 'pleasant residential corner' of suburban Surrey. 'There are no cinemas and the only sign of life of an evening in the tree-lined main shopping street [in New Malden] is the solitary milk bar. It is a quiet place with a first-rate youth record.'

Mark Endean has his father's famous short back lift

Finding entertainment for his two very young children was not a top priority for Russell Endean, but finding a job was. It did not take long. His accountancy qualifications and spotless reputation landed him a position as an auditor with British Petroleum in their Lutyens-designed Britannic House head office in the City of London. He became a Monday-to-Friday commuter taking an early-morning journey that started with a six-minute walk to Worcester Park station, before squeezing into one of the dark-green carriages of the British Rail (Southern Region) slam-door trains that travelled sedately via Motspur Park, Raynes Park, Wimbledon, Earlsfield, Clapham Junction and Vauxhall, arriving almost half an hour later at the Waterloo terminus. Then it was down a steep ramp to join the hordes of bowler-hatted, City workers queuing to board the claustrophobic one-stop Waterloo-and-City line train ('The Drain') to Bank station; followed by a long climb (made easier by the 1960-installed travolator) up to the exit and welcome daylight. Finally there was a brisk ten-minute walk along Moorgate and a right turn into the imposing Finsbury Circus with its incongruous bowling green sitting snugly at its centre. This would be, through freezing fog, snow-on-the-line and muggy summer heatwaves, the former Springbok's hour-long, two-way commute for the next twenty years.

He established with his new employers that he had a life outside the office and that he was not prepared to work over-long hours. He left promptly every day at five and was back home in time to see something of his young family before they went to bed. Daughter Jane remembers him as a caring father. 'Dad managed not only our bedtime stories, but walks, listening to our music, he would recite poetry to us, take me to operas, watch Mark play football at the weekend, play chess and cribbage, and play endless "Test matches" with Ross in the garden, and sometimes the lounge!' His nine-to-five office routine did not seem to affect his standing at BP; as early in 1962 he was sent on a month-long course at The Grange, Hertfordshire, a centre for training senior managers from Britain's leading companies. Then, following time in head office, he moved to BP Chemicals before returning to Brittanic House to specialise in the delicate area of 'Appeals'. During a trip to Port Talbot to audit the books of subsidiary British Hydro Carbon Co. Ltd., and still recognised as a sporting celebrity, Endean told a *Western Mail* reporter that he has 'pleasant memories [of Swansea] but it has changed a lot since 1951. There are so many new buildings now.' Of the match in which Glamorgan beat the South Africans at St Helens, he recalled: 'It was certainly an exciting one. I still remember it well and also the scenes which took place afterwards.'

Early in May 1981, a few days before his fifty-seventh birthday, Endean applied for early retirement – taking advantage of a time when major companies, keen to shed staff, were offering extremely generous pension packages. In his final years he had been working on the many claims against BP, a company that during the 1960s had a reputation for taking on the riskiest ventures and had been responsible for some major environmental disasters, such as the Torrey Canyon oil spill. His value to the company during these tricky times can be judged by a warmly worded, handwritten letter he received on his retirement from the Chairman, Sir David Steel. The boss, not a bad cricketer himself (Oxford Authentics), wrote: 'Everyone agrees that it has been yet another innings during which you have carried your bat with great skill, against some difficult bowling at times.' And he closed by remarking that he was 'personally grateful for your help in many particular cases which we have dealt with, and we all appreciate the overall guidance you have given to this side of BP's developing role in social responsibility.'

****

There would have been much that Russell Endean missed from his previous life in South Africa, but there was compensation in the form of an unparalleled mix of cultural events now on his doorstep. Some theatre and concert programmes in the family archive show that he and Muriel wasted no time in 'going up west' to make frequent use of what London had to offer. They got hot tickets for *Beyond the Fringe* at the Fortune Theatre, an irreverent review performed by Peter Cook, Dudley Moore, Alan Bennett and Jonathan Miller. The series of sketches (mainly written by Cook), performed by the quartet of mid-twenties, Oxbridge-educated men dressed in demure dark-grey suits, cruelly mocked authority and the Establishment in a ground-breaking way. This extract from *Home Thoughts From Abroad* would have had particular resonance for the couple just arrived from South Africa:

> **Bennett**: I think there is a danger though of seeing the colour problem simply in terms of black and white.
> **Cook**: It's a lot more complicated than that.
> **Moore**: I gather the Negroes are sweeping the country.
> **Miller**: They are. It's one of the few jobs they can get.

And it was not long before Russell was pursuing his greatest love: in 1962 he and Muriel saw *Carmen* at Sadlers Wells and *Cavalleria Rusticana* and *Pagliacci* at Covent Garden, followed next year, again at the Royal Opera House, by Tito Gobbi and Geraint Evans in *Don Giovanni*. Conscious of how fortunate he now was to be living a city of high culture, Russell made a point of sending long-playing records, not available in South Africa, back to Ian McDonald, a music-loving friend in Johannesburg.

****

The Endean family quickly settled into a corner of suburbia that by the 1960s had become an attractive location for the affluent middle class. That class now included professional footballers – Jimmy Hill having negotiated on behalf of the PFA (the players' trade union) the end of the maximum wage, which in 1961 was £20 a week. The most famous beneficiary, and first £100-a-week footballer, was Fulham's Johnny Haynes, the stylish inside-forward who sprayed his pin-point passes around Craven Cottage. Two of Haynes' team-mates – George Cohen, future 1966 World Cup winner, and Bobby Robson, England international and in time acclaimed manager of Barcelona and England, became near neighbours of the Endeans. And it was Fulham that Russell, and later his sons Mark and Ross, would call their team. Ross, who had completed the family, was born in St Helier Hospital, Carshalton on 1st December 1966. Endean's salary was high enough to enable him to educate privately his three children, although he was forced to stop funding needy boys at St John's College, an established tradition amongst Old Johannians. Daughter Jane went to Wimbledon High School, while Mark and Ross were pupils at King's College School, Wimbledon. Mark now lives on the Gold Coast of Queensland, where his son Adam plays semi-professional football whilst (like his grandfather before him) is studying to be an accountant. Ross inherited the cricket genes, playing school and club cricket to a high level; he and Russell, to the delight of both, played together on one occasion for MCC at Hurstpierpoint School.

Daughter Jane obtained an M.Sc in metallurgy from Cranfield University and, like her great-grandmother before her, went on to work successfully in a man's world. To the alarm of her father (although he was quietly proud of his pioneering offspring), she took a job at the Harmony Gold Mine in Orange Free State where she was the only female for miles around. On her trips to the local town of Virginia to shop or have a beer, jaws dropped and conversation stopped when she walked in to the local store or bar. Jane was the adventurous one of the family – in her early twenties she did a world tour, and in a surviving letter from the trip she describes her climb to the top of Ayers Rock, where the view was 'magnificent, but my legs felt like jelly when I got to the bottom.' On another trip it was her heart that was fluttering during a 27-hour train journey to Alice Springs. ' I thought of you mum, your first fears were almost realised. I was proposed to by an Aussie footballer travelling to Darwin for their season! I thought – Best I refuse. He was intelligent but so big-headed, measured 6 foot across the shoulders. I thought you'd love it.' After time in Hong Kong where her husband Steve was working, Jane is now back in England, retired and –something else that would have pleased her father – is a fanatical bowls player.

****

Before Russell Endean himself stepped onto the bowling green, he played a lot more cricket. At weekends it was for Malden Wanderers; but he was also a great supporter of MCC matches against schools, playing many times in these fixtures. He also played in four two-day games for the club during the 1960s; in 1962 at Lord's against Ireland, in an unbroken partnership of 184 with Mike Brearley (106 not out), Russell made an undefeated 89. And as a swan song to his first-class career there were two final games: in 1963 he played for MCC at Lord's in a drawn match against Oxford University who were captained by – after his motoring accident – the one-eyed Nawab of Pataudi. On day two of the match, while President Kennedy – less than five months before his assassination – was visiting the home of his Irish ancestors in County Wexford, 'Tiger' Pataudi, down at number eight for the Dark Blues, 'made 26 with six beautiful scoring shots, one six and five fours, from two hooks, a late cut, a square-cut, a cover-drive and an off-drive.' *The Times* went on to record a 'fine partnership between the South African Endean and [Denis] Compton.' The correspondent concentrated on the batting of the Lord's favourite who 'produced every stroke from his vast range … when he was out for 87 made in 115 minutes, with 11 fours and three sixes he was cheered all the way back to the pavilion.' The final sentence of the report merely added: 'Endean made 106 not out (14 fours).' The former Springbok, with his mastery of placement, would have been happy to rotate the strike and play second fiddle to the maestro.

Malden Wanderers Cricket Club
Alec Stewart named it one of his 10 favourite grounds

Malden Wanderers 1962
Standing: Tom Skinner (umpire), John Gaskell, Mike Stone,
Mike Elliott, Giles Mason, Keith Venables, Ray Budd
Seated: Pat Ransom, Michael Burns, Harry Edney,
Russell Endean, John Walters, Brian Gidney

Endean's last first-class match was played the following summer at Castle Avenue, Dublin against Ireland. Opening the batting he scored 26 and 12, and, despite legendary Irish hospitality, was still sharp enough to make two stumpings – one off George Chesterton, the former Worcestershire medium-pacer who had been the first bowler to dismiss Endean on the 1951 tour. So on 8 September 1964 ended a 19-year first-class career. The final tally being: 134 matches; 230 innings; 25 not outs; 7757 runs; 247 highest score; 37.83 average, with 15 centuries and 34 fifties. He took 158 catches and made 13 stumpings; and he also bowled 102 balls, taking 2 wickets for 73.

Endean's weekend cricket was played for Malden Wanderers – his membership being approved at a committee meeting on 23 August 1961 by chairman Cecil Tredwell (Russell's brother-in-law) who agreed to a reduced subscription of two guineas, as he was not 'playing a full season's cricket'. Preferring to keep work and leisure separate, Russell had chosen to play for his local team rather than for Lensbury, the BP/Shell club that had extensive manicured facilities at Teddington Lock. Malden had started as a small nomadic village club in 1879, but by the time Endean joined in 1961 it was one of the leading clubs in London. The South African having quickly made his mark at the Wanderers; in 1963 he was elected captain of the 1st XI. He started his campaign as skipper with a late April century at Guildford, and finished the season top of the Malden Wanderers averages (750 runs at 49.11).

Four days after England had beaten West Germany 4-2 in the 1966 World Cup final, Malden Wanderers found themselves struggling to raise a strong side for a prestigious mid-week fixture against Surrey Club & Ground (an XI made up of amateurs and young professionals that played clubs around the County). Russell Endean, knowing that three young South Africans touring with the Wilfred Isaacs team were looking for a game, invited them to play as guests for the Wanderers. When it was being decided who should bat first (done by gentlemanly negotiation rather than the spin of a coin), Surrey's amateur, big-wig captain, Bertie Joel, asked Malden skipper-for-the-day John Cope if any stars like Sir Leonard Hutton, Richard Hutton or Russell Endean were playing. John said no, so Bertie said you can 'win the toss'. Cope, a PE teacher who went on to become a highly successful and pioneering director of cricket development at Nottinghamshire CCC, thanked him and invited Surrey to bat first. The Club & Ground struggled to 199-7 in 57 overs; one of the South Africans, Mike Procter, took 4-51 in twenty overs, and another, Lee Irvine, claimed three victims behind the stumps, including a brilliant diving catch off Procter to dismiss Younis Ahmed (future Pakistan Test player) for 0. For Surrey, Mike Hooper made 69 and Mike Willett 65. Malden were left 2 hours 40 minutes batting, during which time they received a tardily-delivered 41 overs. Geoff Arnold quickly reduced the Wanderers to 31-3 – at which point Barry Richards was joined by Procter and together they scored 150 in the next 77 minutes, Richards making 54, Procter 96 (Irvine had earlier made 25). After the three 'guests' were dismissed, wickets tumbled and, when Arnold began the last over, eight were still needed for an unlikely Malden victory. But two of their club's second XI bowlers, Graham Laurie and David Cowan, with an edged four, and some scrambled singles, including one off the last ball, won the match. And when Bertie Joel shook hands with the Wanderers' skipper at the end of the game, he said: 'I think you pulled a fast one on me today, John.' Three days later the three South Africans, along with Richard Hutton and Russell Endean, played for Malden in a Saturday fixture against Beddington. Chasing 167, the star-studded team, containing five former or future Test players, lost by 82 runs, being dismissed for an embarrassing 85 – with the quintet making 45 between them.

Fixtures between London clubs had always been played on a 'friendly' basis, but this was not to say that there were not long-standing rivalries, or that the cricket was always soft. Recalling another match against Beddington, John Cope for the only time saw Russell Endean become angry on the cricket field. On a slow and low pitch, he was struggling to push the score along, which led to some unpleasant sneering from a young Surrey cricketer fielding at short-leg. This did not go down well with a man who had repelled the best that Miller, Lindwall, Tyson and Statham had to offer, and the former Springbok gave an uncharacteristically blunt response to the mocking of the very average county player.

The traditional non-competitive nature of cricket amongst Surrey's leading clubs was to change forever in the 1960s. Led by former Surrey, Northamptonshire and England batsman, the Streatham-born Raman Subba Row, it was proposed that a league system be formed in the county. Although the Club Cricket Conference accepted knock-out competitions such as the Kemp's Cup, somewhat illogically it bitterly opposed this radical change of direction. CCC secretary Major Woods described it as 'this terrible subject of league cricket' and threatened the rebel clubs with expulsion. His stance was supported by sections of the press: 'Whatever euphemism is used to overcome the sinful word "league" the intention clearly is that clubs should play for points and cups instead of pleasure and pints,' wrote Doug Ibbotson in the *Evening News*. 'It puts an edge on the game alright but instead of playing to win or not to lose, you play to win and not to lose at all costs.' Although they would eventually have to change their minds, some of the socially exclusive clubs in Surrey – Esher, Reigate Priory, Bank of England and Wimbledon amongst them – refused to be part of the new league. But despite this boycott of the blue-bloods, the Surrey Championship became a reality and played its first fixtures in the summer of 1968.

Nearly fifty years later and now supported by the ECB, there are numerous leagues across the whole of the South of England – a development that Endean, having been brought up on weekend league and cup cricket in Johannesburg, would have approved of. The introduction of structured competitive cricket in Surrey convinced him that at forty-four he would continue playing. And his presence in the early years of the Surrey Championship helped to establish the league, a contribution that was recognised by a picture of the South African on the front cover along with an accompanying article about him in the 1976 *Year Book*. Always wearing his now fading green South Africa cap, he played on for the first nine years of the new league (in 1975 and '76 as Malden's captain) and was consistently one of the Championship's leading run scorers, finishing with a league aggregate of 3,160 runs at 38.41. He also took 44 catches and made 6 stumpings. Ross Endean tells how even when Russell was in his late fifties preparation for matches was still important – he would get his young son to give him forty or fifty catches in the back garden before he went off to play in a Saturday afternoon Surrey Championship game.

Russell Endean was a highly respected cricketer at Malden Wanderers. The young club players felt privileged to be playing alongside him, even though occasionally being quietly told to calm down, as no doubt he had told Neil Adcock or Hugh Tayfield when these two combatives lost their rags playing for Transvaal and South Africa. Although occasionally struggling on poorly prepared club pitches, he scored memorable centuries on grounds used for first-class cricket such as Hastings, Guildford and at Horsham's Cricketfield Road ground – where Malden Wanderers' swing bowler and former National Theatre director Michael Elliott remembers Russell driving the opposition to distraction by consistently threading the ball through the ever-increasing number of fielders posted in the covers. Another former Wanderers' player, Howard Townson, has a vivid memory of Endean batting in an evening limited-overs cup game for Malden on an unpredictable council wicket against Surbiton Hill Methodists. Townson was impressed that the former Springbok 'who had played on nearly all the great grounds around the world, was still prepared to guts it out on a rock-hard, bumpy wicket at Surbiton's Victoria Road Rec., getting behind the line as though it were a Test match while all around him batsmen were backing away from the rearing deliveries on the spiteful pitch.' Jazz bass-player David Miles remembers the uplifting vignette of Russell (in his late 50s) bowling for long spells to diminutive colts in the Malden nets; and Kenyan Asian Stephen Nunes, who arrived in England in 1961, tells how he was taken under Endean's wing at the Wanderers' nets and told to 'cut out the hook shot as the ball keeps lower than in Africa.' At a dinner to celebrate twenty years with the Wanderers, Russell was presented with a tankard by Club president Iain Reid who said:

Malden Wanderers Centenary dinner, 1979
Left to right: Endean, Doug Insole, Giles Mason, Micky Stewart,
Les Hewitt, Graham Roope, John Cope, Tony Till

'He is a tremendously warm-hearted character and no one need ever be afraid of asking for help or advice as he is always only too willing to give it'. The former Springbok replied: 'I have had twenty very happy years at Malden. It has been a bonus, because when I first came to England I thought I had come to the end of my cricketing career.'

As well as Saturday club cricket, Russell Endean had a real commitment to supporting cricket in schools, playing four or five out-matches for MCC every year. Such fixtures were not likely to encourage cricket at say Tolworth Secondary Modern since the list was made up almost exclusively of England's public schools. Endean during the 1960s and 1970s played games against schools such as Radley, Harrow, Bradfield, King's College Wimbledon, Douai Abbey and Eton. These MCC teams, that usually had a number of Lord's ground-staff boys brought along to score the runs and take the wickets, also included such luminaries as Ian MacLaurin, future boss of Tesco and the chairman of the England & Wales Cricket Board; and Aidan Crawley, first editor-in-chief of Independent Television News and, at different times, MP for both the Labour and Conservative parties. Endean continued to play for the MCC in schools matches until 1980 when, in his last season at the age of 56, he made 257 runs in eight innings.

Russell also had frequent requests to play in charity matches. One such was a 1970 Sunday game at Northwood in aid of Imperial Cancer Research, to which he took his autograph-hunting daughter. 'To Jane with love Cliff Morgan' was one inscription on the match-day scorecard. Other rugby internationals in the Ruckers Club XI were Dickie Jeeps, Jeff Butterfield and Chris Winn as well as sports commentator Neil Durden-Smith. The scorecard noted that 'The "Lucky Draw" will be made by Miss Judith Chalmers [Mrs Durden-Smith] during the Tea Interval.' In another match, in 1971, Endean played at Lord's for a star-studded MCC team that included former England players: Reg Simpson, Derek Shackleton, Alan Oakman and Sir Leonard Hutton in a game in aid of the Len Muncer (Glamorgan) and Harry Sharp (Middlesex) Testimonial – the MCC's long-standing head and assistant head coaches at Lord's. In appreciation of his feats as a Test cricketer, and later for his commitment to all forms of the game, but particularly of cricket in schools, in 1966 he received a letter from former first-class cricketer and Conservative Prime Minister, Sir Alec Douglas Home who, in his capacity as President invited Endean to become a life member of MCC.

Although Endean would not have played much hockey in his second season in England when the Thames froze over during the 'Big Freeze' of 1962/63, on winter Saturdays the former South African international turned out for the Mid Surrey H.C 1st XI. This strong London club's home games were played – in the days before the introduction of leagues and artificial pitches – on the grass outfield of the Malden Wanderers' Cambridge Avenue ground. The two most famous Mid Surrey players were England internationals Dickie Deluth; and the silkily-skilled forward, the Nagpur-born John Conroy (also a talented cricketer) who represented Great Britain in the Helsinki Olympics in 1952, winning a bronze medal, and again at the 1956 Olympics in Melbourne.

****

Although far from home, Endean was still remembered. He received a great deal of mail from South Africa, including a 1966 letter from former Johannesburg work colleague Paul Gardner that, as well as discussing African politics, was also full of juicy titbits of gossip: 'Blackwell is supplementing his pension by assisting to manage the Westville Hotel but we hear he has again started to help boost the bar sales!!' And of E.L., 'he is doing a sterling job as captain of the golf club for the second year – not the slightest visible sign of even a nibble of a romance with him but he's a silent worker we know that.' But Gardner goes on to write that the hottest topic of conversation amongst his friends is Southern Rhodesia, noting that they were 'either praising [Ian] Smith's courage or questioning his sanity in risking a war with the black states whilst so many of his internal problems remain unsolved … the whole business has certainly resulted in some pretty hard things being said about Harold Wilson & Britain in general.' Gardner finishes his long letter more personally: 'Everywhere I go in SA I am asked for news of you, so you needn't think you have been forgotten.'

Russell's parents were also regular letter writers on thin, blue, airmail notepaper. A 1967 letter from his father (who always addressed him as 'Russ') sends everyday news about sport ('Old Joes have a tough game against West Rand this weekend') and how he was coping while the family servant was on holiday: 'Wilson is away for a couple of weeks, so I am learning how to make beds, cook a rasher of bacon and do sundry household chores, never too late to learn even if one is on the verge of 79. Much love to you all, Dad.' In one particularly poignant letter from Russell's mother dated 2 May 1979 – written only days before her death – she remembers meeting her soldier fiancé in London after he had been hit by shrapnel in the 'Last Big Push' of 1918. 'When he was well enough he took me out – in his blue (wounded warrior) suit for a few hours daily.' In the same letter she has praise for her grandchild's academic progress ('very interested to have Ross's report to read, and think it is as good as ever'); and welcomes a recent development in British politics ('We saw Mrs Thatcher just after she had won the election. She is certainly a lovely person to look at and she has brains, common sense, also capable of hard work – she should do well as P.M.').

The Endean parents were regular visitors to England, and Russell's father was very much at home with a pint of Worthington in the 'Men's Only Bar' at Malden Wanderers Cricket Club. There were also many visits to the UK by touring teams from South Africa during the 1960s – as well as the Wilfred Issacs XI, other teams who made the trip were South African Universities; the Kookaburras from Durban; the Sabres (University of Cape Town); and the Wanderers Club from Johannesburg (Russell, playing for Public School Wanderers at Godalming, scored a century against these tourists). Because of intense international criticism of such events as the Sharpeville massacre followed by the Rivonia treason trial of Nelson Mandela and others, these all-white visiting teams had to keep a very low profile. To allay some of the expected disapproval, one 1984 visiting team, Union CC from Port Elizabeth, brought along a dressed-in-white, but non-playing, token black man.

In an article about a 1966 tour of Old Johannians (Endean had formed the London branch of the OJs), Geoff Poulton describes a rendezvous in London with the always wistful-for-Johannesburg host: 'As we alighted from the taxi he came forward to greet us. His hair was a little greyer perhaps, but otherwise he hadn't changed in five years. His athletic build had not turned to fat and he still walked on his toes like a panther, as though ready to spring into action at any moment. It was the Russell of old.' On a taxi ride he showed the visitors some of the traditional sights – Buckingham Palace, Trafalgar Square and Downing Street – but the attraction that most caught the attention of the young South Africans was London's 'undeniable claims to being the mini-skirt capital of the world.' The article finishes by hinting at what a very great deal their hero had given up when he migrated to England, and how much he was missed back in South Africa. 'At Green Park the taxi stopped and Russell left us to return to his office. He gave a final wave and started off down the pavement. To us he was Russell Endean, the club's only double Springbok who had given so much to the Old Johannians. Then as the taxi gathered momentum, he disappeared among the crowds to become again just one of the teeming millions of London.'

After establishing himself and his family in England, Russell by the late 1960s was travelling back to Johannesburg almost every other year, these journeys were made principally to see his by now aging parents. During a month-long trip in 1967, accompanied by his older son Mark, Russell fitted in a game for Old Johannians. 'It's just wonderful being back home and playing cricket in sunny December weather,' he told a *Rand Daily Mail* reporter. On meatier matters – as to whether Basil D'Oliveira would be permitted to play against the Springboks in the forthcoming tour – Endean's opinion was unequivocal: 'Dolly is a certainty for selection. Mr Vorster's statement earlier this year that non-Whites would be allowed to play against South Africa was well received in England, and the door has been left open for Dolly to come out.'

The MCC's and Vorster's U-turns that resulted in the fiasco of the 'D'Oliveira Affair'; and the subsequent cancellation of South Africa's tour to England in 1970, prompted a lengthy Endean letter to *The Times*. For a man who normally held his cards tightly to his chest (his children never knew which way he cast his vote at election times), he expressed some heartfelt views: 'During the war my parents, along with countless thousands of other South Africans, threw open their home to the British troops in South Africa. Virtually to a man the country's cricketers joined in the fight against Hitler; all were volunteers for there was no conscription in South Africa.' The forty-six-year-old Endean, who had been one such volunteer, went on to say that while the situation was 'highly complex' and that the solutions were far from obvious, 'I wonder whether the non-whites would want a multi-racial tour; they could well prefer their own tour in the same way that India and Pakistan tour separately.' He concludes that the cancellation 'will not influence the South African Government's policies – it will only harden the attitude of all shades of opinion against Britain, and even my dear Dad will now think twice about buying British.'

When in 1985 a team from Endean's old school visited England, he organised a trip to Lord's for the boys. This tour took place 'shortly after

State president PW Botha had declared a state of emergency, during which the security forces unleashed a vicious crackdown on the mass democratic movement,' writes Daniel Pretorious in his history of St John's College cricket, and 'because of the prevailing sporting boycott of South African teams, the tour was kept undercover to offset political interference.' Pretorious quotes the College headmaster WW Macfarlane from the tour brochure (a copy preserved in the Endean archive), who recalls sitting in The Parks watching Oxford University playing the South Africans in 1960, the idyllic scene spoiled by 'an anti-apartheid demonstration by a handful of scruffy-looking demonstrators.' Having got that off his chest, and more on message, the head finishes by saying that 'if our tour builds bridges we will have achieved something well worthwhile.' Earlier in 1985 Macfarlane, who must have had some serious doubts about his invitation, welcomed Nobel Peace prizewinner, the Bishop of Johannesburg and Visitor to St John's College, the Rt Rev Desmond Tutu, to a day at the school. But as Pretorious notes the little cleric's 'warmth, humanity and sense of humour had endeared him to all.' For his trouble, the Headmaster received visits from the security police, who wanted to know whether the Bishop was attempting to politicise the school.

The family at Jane's wedding in 1987
left to right: Mark, Muriel, Jane, Russell, Ross

One of Endean's most enjoyable trips back home was in 1989 as a guest of the SACU who were commemorating a hundred years of South African cricket. President Joe Pamensky wrote to Russell to say that the Association were 'truly honoured to have you as a guest' for the 15 days of celebration that included events in Cape Town, Johannesburg and Port Elizabeth (the Currie Cup Final). During this extended visit he was honoured by St John's College for his 'contribution to sport in South Africa and his unwavering loyalty to the school' On a sun-kissed, late-summer's day, the prep school's cricket ground was named the 'Russell Endean Field'.

The Endean Field,
opened in 1989

Later in 1989, when a continued UN arms embargo and trade sanctions, were forcing cracks to appear in the apartheid edifice, South Africa was still in total isolation throughout international sport, Endean again wrote to Fleet Street – this time to the *Daily Telegraph* in defence of the 1983/4 rebel West Indian tourists who had been attacked by award-winning sports writer Michael Calvin. Having seen them play on one of his regular visits back home, he felt that the West Indies team's 'outstanding ability, demeanour and sportsmanship could not have failed to make considerable impact on all sections of the community.' He cited the example of the UK and the USA, where sport 'has offered a lifeline for black people to express themselves', and finished by insisting that 'it is wrong to deny South Africa this lifeline and deprive young people of the right to compete internationally merely because they were born in South Africa.' While these words reflect the moral complexity of Endean's views on separate development, two letters he received from dyed-in-the-wool reactionaries that are retained in the family's archive, show that there were still unreconstructed supporters of apartheid lurking in the backwoods. 'Little pleasure can be derived by playing cricket in the West Indies, India or Pakistan,' asserted Banbury solicitor Denis Coleman. 'There is the racist attitude in all three countries, together with riots, dubious umpiring, and, in Asia, illness. We have given in to blackmail by the coloured countries ... matches against these countries would not have been of great importance.' Major Tony Gay, writing from Rye, congratulated Endean on his letter, 'I couldn't agree with you more. How fallible are politicos!!!'

In 1989 president P.W. Botha was pressured into stepping aside in favor of F.W. de Klerk. De Klerk's government, in negotiation with the Nelson Mandela-led ANC, repealed the Population Registration Act, along with most of the other legislation that formed the legal basis for apartheid. A new constitution, which enfranchised blacks and other racial groups, took effect in 1994, and elections that year led to a coalition government with a non-white majority, marking the official end of the apartheid system.

****

In his late fifties Endean played less cricket both for MCC and Malden Wanderers, although he had had one last hurrah at the Oval – at the age of fifty-four playing (and keeping wicket) for the club in the semi-final and final of the Decca Cup, a six-a-side tournament for London teams. Instead it was to a new sport that his interest turned. A ten-minute walk from his home, Malden & Coombe Bowling Club, situated in a picturesque corner of the council-owned Manor Park, has a secluded green with only the Raynes Park-to-Chessington branch line running alongside to disturb its tranquillity. There he joined another former international, 1930s Wimbledon speedway rider Claude Rye, who turned to the bowling green once his dirt-track days were over.

One of the reasons Endean made the switch, he told fellow-bowler Ted Godley, was that apart from his aging limbs, it was that in club cricket he was 'always expected to score runs', whereas as a bowler he was starting from scratch. For hours alone on one of the empty rinks, he assiduously practised his new sport and even spent time polishing the all-important delivery action in his back garden. He quickly became a skilled bowler, in no time playing in matches; and in 1987 he won his first club singles competition – the first of many finals he was to appear in over the next fourteen years. Not content with just playing, he obtained a coaching qualification and became the club's official coach. Tony Josolyne, whom he taught to play, remembers Russell as very quiet but highly professional in his approach to teaching. Tony says he was also a fine player who was exceptionally good when it came to attacking a particular wood; and he often acted as an encouraging skipper, applauding a good bowl with a discreet little clap. Daughter Jane says that her father's one regret in his new-found sport was that he never obtained his Surrey Badge. He came close but was up against some exceptionally good players during the 1980s and '90s including the eternally pipe-smoking international, David Bryant. Many of Russell's fellow bowlers were former club cricketers and liked to engage him about the game. He was happy to do so, including analysing Compton's technique for the sweep ('the bat coming down on the ball and hitting behind square'); and, when hearing that David Gower was being touted as the best left-hander ever, Russell asked: 'What about my little friend Neil Harvey?' But one subject Godley recalls was off-limits was the 'handling-the-ball' incident: 'He just didn't want to talk about it.'

William Endean

During the 1970s Russell lost both his parents. His father William Endean died in Johannesburg in 1975, aged 87. His long life had taken him from the tin mines of Cornwall to the rich seams of the Witwatersrand gold fields, followed by distinguished First World War service – he was part of the South African Brigade that was engaged in the bloody battle for Delville Wood during the Battle of the Somme. Back in Johannesburg he held a senior management position with Consolidated Goldfields for many years, before enjoying a contented retirement that included daily visits to the sanctuary of the Old Johannian's bowling green.

His wife Ella died at home in 1979 (a few days later her aged servant Wilson also died). In a long letter to Russell, his brother told how, after her fall, she 'slipped away' before the ambulance arrived. In her will she gave half of her considerable assets to older son Howard, while the other half was divided equally between Russell, Muriel, Mark, Jane and Ross.

One of the great delights of playing bowls for Russell Endean was that it was a passion that he could share with his wife. Muriel decided that having been a 'cricket widow' for many years, she was not going to be a 'bowls widow' as well. She followed her husband onto the rinks with some gusto and no little ability, joining the Manor Park Ladies BC that played on the same green that was used by Russell's club. From the photographs in the club's collection it is obvious that, whether away on a tour to Devon or at a club dance, this was a happy time for them both – bowls had become a late-flowering bond in their marriage. With the children grown up, Muriel and Russell made frequent trips back to South Africa where they could both play at the Old Johannians Club – a cliquey, male-dominated environment that in her younger days Muriel had found such an unwelcoming place. Still news thirty-two years after he left home, Endean in 1993 on a 'Friends of Springboks' bowls tour with Muriel was interviewed by the *Cape Argus*. 'He is just as sprightly at 68 as he was when a hero on the cricket and hockey fields,' reported Alan Simmonds, 'an infectious smile is still there and the lithe frame carries no fat. "I loosen up from time

136

Muriel and Russell with friends in Johannesburg, 1993

to time but should do more.'" The husband-and-wife bowlers had enjoyed twenty years of retirement, including these regular returns to the Union, before cancer of the colon ended Muriel's life very suddenly in 2001.

Even before Muriel's death, Russell was showing signs of his own decline. Malden bowlers remembered noticing the first signs of a failing memory – in 1999 he turned up for a match with only three of his four bowls. As his memory loss became worse, and because he was also suffering, like his father before him, from Parkinson's disease, he was forced to move to nearby Surbiton to live with his older son Mark who, along with his other son Ross, unstintingly cared for their father for the last years of his life. In 2002, to relieve the two sons of their burden, Russell went out to Hong Kong at the invitation of his daughter Jane. In his three-month stay he had the joy of watching his grandchildren play hockey in Happy Valley and even managed to play stationary table tennis with them. But although there were some light-hearted moments – he would wander off and be found miles away from where he was returned home, thanks to a map and phone-number in his pocket – his character was being changed out of all recognition by his two cruel illnesses. And, on the 28 June, the same day that the touring South Africans were playing a one-day international against the old enemy England at the Oval, one of the Springboks' greatest cricketing sons died aged 79 at Kingston upon Thames. A town many miles from his spiritual home – and where in the same local hospital, thirteen years earlier, his old Yorkshire adversary Sir Leonard Hutton had also passed away.

Epilogue

A True Gentleman

When news of Russell Endean's death filtered through to the touring South Africans during their one-day international against Zimbabwe at the St Lawrence Ground, Canterbury, they were quick to offer their condolences and to acknowledge the passing of one of their former champions. 'It's always sad when a highly respected player passes away,' said their coach Eric Simons, recalling him as 'part of a wonderful era when South Africa was a major force in Test cricket'.

A Service of Thanksgiving and Remembrance was held at Randall's Park Crematorium Chapel, Leatherhead at which his granddaughter, Jennifer Ellis, played the violin and daughter Jane gave a moving tribute: 'My father, Russell Endean, was a true gentleman. My dictionary defines gentleman as "a man of chivalrous instincts, of fine feelings and of good breeding". I believe my father was all this and more.' She went on to say that 'Dad gave his complete attention to whatever he did, and whomever he met … as a father I cannot fault him in any way whatsoever.' Jane finished by talking a little of her father's decline that 'was not easy for him or for us to accept. Mark and Ross have shown extraordinary compassion, perseverance, integrity, kindness and patience in respect of Dad's wishes. If only Dad could have recognised these actions of his sons, I am sure this would be his greatest ever source of pride.'

The Surrey funeral, which was attended mainly by the Endean family and English friends, was followed, at Russell's express wish, by a scattering of his ashes at St John's College. Jane, Mark and Ross travelled to Johannesburg for the 14 October memorial service that took place at 4 pm on a gloriously clear-blue, high-veld spring day. After Russell's ashes had been interred in the College's Garden of Remembrance, the first minister, Mike Arnold, conducted the service in the College chapel. He said that from his 'cricket-crazed teenage years', he could remember every catch that his hero Russell Endean took at the Wanderers. There were over 50 people in the congregation, amongst them former Springboks John Waite, Roy McLean and Clive Rice. There were also six of the 1936 St John's Junior School football team present; the four missing had all died in the Second World War. Jane Endean gave a tribute to he father, followed by Clive Macdonald, an Old Johannian who spoke of the years after the war before the family left for England. He remembered those carefree days when Russell was single: 'living with friends in Jo'burg, sharing houses, ripping up orchards for a football pitch in the garden; asking people to walk home from work when the day's practice was cancelled, and oversleeping on the day he was due to go on tour.'

The obituaries from England and South Africa that followed Russell Endean's death were uniform in their praise for the man, and nearly all pursued similar themes. *The Times* described him as 'a thinking cricketer who ironically made most headlines for two of the more bizarre dismissals [obstructing the field and 'handling the ball'] in Test cricket'. All mentioned the (warm) Australian 'Endless' tag that was to stick; his reputation as a world-class fielder; and his apotheosis, the 1952/3 tour of Australasia. But above all, they were unanimous in their assessment of his character. 'Quiet, undemonstrative and soft-spoken, Endean was universally popular, within and outside the game,' was the *Daily Telegraph*'s view. From South Africa, Roy McLean wrote: 'Russell had such a huge heart, he was a complete cricketer.' And the sentiment of Charles Fortune was shared by all who knew him and was also quoted in the *Wisden* obituary: 'Whatever the passport is to be a gentleman, Russell had that passport.'

William Russell Endean

Born: Johannesburg, 31 May 1924

Died: Kingston-upon-Thames, 28 June 2003

BATTING AND FIELDING IN TEST CRICKET

Year		M	I	NO	Runs	HS	Ave	Ct
1951	v Eng (a)	1	2	0	38	31	19.00	3
1952/53	v Aus (a)	5	10	1	438	162*	48.66	9
1952/53	v NZ (a)	2	3	1	204	116	102.00	4
1953/54	v Aus (h)	5	8	1	293	93	41.85	9
1955	v Eng (a)	5	10	1	246	116*	27.33	0
1956/57	v Eng (h)	5	10	0	158	70	15.80	10
1957/58	v Aus (h)	5	9	0	253	77	28.11	6
TOTAL		**28**	**52**	**4**	**1630**	**162***	**33.95**	**41**

CENTURIES IN TEST CRICKET

162* v Australia, Melbourne, 1952

116 v New Zealand, Auckland, 1953

116* v England, Headingley, 1955

BATTING AND FIELDING IN ALL FIRST-CLASS CRICKET

M	I	NO	Runs	HS	Ave	100s	Ct	St
134	**230**	**25**	**7757**	**247**	**37.83**	**15**	**158**	**13**

DOUBLE CENTURIES IN FIRST-CLASS CRICKET

235 Transvaal v Orange Free State, Johannesburg, 1954/55

247 Transvaal v Eastern Province, Johannesburg, 1955/56

204* Transvaal v Border, Johannesburg, 1959/60

Bibliography

Barker, Ralph: *Ten Great Innings* (Chatto & Windus, 1964)

Bassano, Brian: *South African Cricket Volume IV 1947-1960* (Cricket Connections International, 1996)

Benaud, Richie: *Anything but … An Autobiography* (Hodder & Stoughton, 1998)

Cheetham, Jack: *Caught by the Springboks* (Hodder and Stoughton, 1954)

Cheetham, Jack: *I Declare*, Howard Timmins (Cape Town, 1956)

Duffus, Louis: *Cricketers of the Veld* (Sampson Low, 1947)

Evans, Godfrey: *Action in Cricket* (The Sportsman's Book Club, 1957)

Ferguson, W.H.: *Mr Cricket, The Autobiography of WH Ferguson BEM* (Nicholas Kaye, 1957)

Fortune, Charles: *The MCC Tour of South Africa 1956-1957* (George Harrap, 1957)

Gordon, Gerald: *Let the Day Perish* (Methuen, 1952)

Hutton, Len: *Fifty Years in Cricket* (Stanley Paul, 1984)

Insole, Douglas: *Cricket in the Middle* (Heinemann, 1960)

Kahn, Roger: *The Boys of Summer* (Narperperennial, New York, 1987)

Kynaston, David: *Family Britain 1951-57* (Bloomsbury, 2009)

Kynaston, David: *Modernity Britain 1959-62* (Bloomsbury, 2014)

McLean, Roy: *Sackcloth Without Ashes* (Howard Timmins, Cape Town, 1958)

Medworth, C.O.: *Noursemen in England* (Werner Laurie, 1952)

Moyes, A.G.: *The South Africans in Australia 1952-1953* (George G. Harrap & Co Ltd., 1953)

Oborne, Peter: *Basil D'Oliveira, Cricket and Conspiracy: The Untold Story* (Little Brown, 2004)

Orpen, Neil: *Victory in Italy – South African Forces World War II (Vol. V)* (Purnell, Cape Town, 1975)

Perry, Roland: *Keith Miller* (Aurum, 2006)

Pretorious, Daniel: *A History of Cricket at St John's College, Johannesburg* (unpublished)

Quelch, Tim: *Bent Arms & Dodgy Wickets* (Pitch Publishing, 2012)

Ross, Alan: *Cape Summer* (Hamish Hamilton, 1957)

Sheppard, David: *Parson's Pitch* (Hodder & Stoughton, 1964)

van Ryneveld, Clive: *20th Century All-Rounder* (Pretext, Cape Town, 2011)

Waite, John: *Perchance To Bowl* (Nicholas Kaye, 1961)

Playfair Annuals 1951-5
Wisden Almanack, various

Newspapers and periodicals are as acknowledged in the text

INDEX